**DK** **SMITHSO**

T0113073

# QUIZ
## YOURSELF
## CLEVER!

# ANIMALS
## OF THE WORLD

Produced for DK by Just Content Limited
10A Little Square, Braintree, Essex, CM7 1UT
**Editorial** Just Content Limited
**Design** PDQ Digital Media Solutions, Bungay, UK

**Senior editor** Shaila Brown
**Senior US editor** Megan Douglass
**Senior art editor** Jacqui Swan
**Managing Editor** Rachel Fox
**Managing art editor** Owen Peyton Jones
**Production editor** Gillian Reid
**Production controller** Laura Andrews
**Jacket designer** Vidushi Chaudhry
**DTP designer** Deepak Mittal
**Senior jackets coordinator** Priyanka Sharma Saddi
**Jacket design development manager** Sophia MTT
**Publisher** Andrew Macintyre
**Associate publishing director** Liz Wheeler
**Art director** Karen Self
**Publishing director** Jonathan Metcalf

First American Edition, 2024
Published in the United States by DK Publishing,
a Division of Penguin Random House LLC
1745 Broadway, 20th Floor, New York, NY 10019

A catalog record for this book
is available from the Library of Congress.
ISBN: 978-0-5938-4150-1

DK books are available at special discounts when purchased in bulk
for sales promotions, premiums, fund-raising, or educational use.
For details, contact: DK Publishing Special Markets,
1745 Broadway, 20th Floor, New York, NY 10019
SpecialSales@dk.com

Printed and bound in China

www.dk.com

The name of the Smithsonian Institution and the sunburst logo
are registered trademarks of the Smithsonian Institution.
For more information, please visit www.si.edu

Smithsonian

# Contents

# How to use this book

One of the best ways to test your knowledge is by doing quizzes. It's also a fun way to learn new facts. You can do the quizzes by yourself, with a friend, or in teams.

## How to play

Try answering the questions on the right-hand page. You'll find all the answers on the next page. How many questions did you get right? If you want to increase your scores and boost your brain power, re-read the profile and test yourself again! If you are playing with friends, you'll need pen and paper to write down the answers. Whoever gets the most correct answers wins!

A description of the animal at the top of the page provides a clue.

### ?? Ghost of the mountains ??

What **animal** is this?

Is it **endangered**?

What does it **eat**?

What is this animal's natural **habitat**?

Is it a **social creature**?

How does it hunt down its **prey**?

These are the questions about the animal.

The animal shown in the photograph is normally an adult.

**Mammals**
*Panthera uncia*

13

The animal's common name is revealed on the next page.

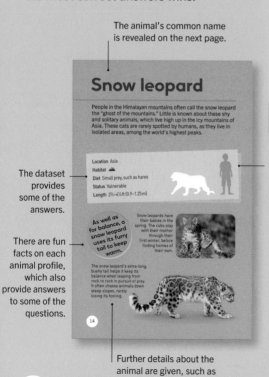

### Snow leopard

People in the Himalayan mountains often call the snow leopard the "ghost of the mountains." Little is known about these shy and solitary animals, which live high up in the icy mountains of Asia. These cats are rarely spotted by humans, as they live in isolated areas, among the world's highest peaks.

Location Asia
Habitat ⛰
Diet Small prey, such as hares
Status Vulnerable
Length 2¾–4¼ft (0.9–1.25m)

As well as for balance, a snow leopard uses its furry tail to keep warm.

Snow leopards have their babies in the spring. The cubs stay with their mother through their first winter, before finding homes of their own.

The snow leopard's extra-long, bushy tail helps it keep its balance when leaping from rock to rock in pursuit of prey. It often chases animals down steep slopes, rarely losing its footing.

14

Scale graphics are included to give an idea of the animal's size compared to a child.

The animal group and the species' Latin name appears at the bottom of the page to help you guess the animal's identity.

The dataset provides some of the answers.

There are fun facts on each animal profile, which also provide answers to some of the questions.

Further details about the animal are given, such as behavior, habitat, and diet.

# Measurements and symbols

**Scale measurements** give a useful size comparison.

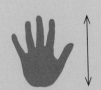

**Child =**
57 in (145 cm) tall

**Hand =**
6 in (16 cm) long

**Thumb =**
1⅓ in (3.5 cm) long

---

## Habitat symbols show the animal's natural environment.

 Temperate forest

Coniferous forest

Tropical forest, rainforest

Mountains, highlands

Urban areas, parks, gardens

 Wetlands, lakes, swamps

Coastal areas, beaches, cliffs

Rivers, streams

Polar regions, tundra

Coral reefs

Open habitats, savanna, fields

Mangrove swamps

Seas, oceans

Desert, semi-desert

---

## The **length** gives a measurement of the adult animal.

**Reptiles:**
Length of carapace (shell) for tortoises and turtles; head and body, including tail, for all other species.

**Fish & Amphibians:**
Head and body, including tail.

**Mammals:**
Head and body (not including tail).

**Birds:**
Tip of bill to tip of tail.

**Invertebrates & Insects:**
Wingspan for winged insects, head and body for all other species.

# The IUCN Red List

The dataset provides the status of each animal, taken from The IUCN (International Union for Conservation of Nature) Red List of Threatened Species™. They have assessed the threats to many species, and given them a category that describes their risk of extinction.

The categories are explained here.

- **Not Evaluated** Data not yet assessed against the five IUCN criteria.

- **Data Deficient** Not a threat category. Population and distribution data is insufficient for assessment.

- **Least Concern** Low-risk category that includes widespread and common species.

- **Near Threatened** Strong possibility of becoming endangered in the near future.

- **Vulnerable** Facing a high risk of extinction in the wild.

- **Endangered** Strong possibility of extinction in the wild in the near future.

- **Critically Endangered** Facing an extremely high risk of extinction in the wild in the immediate future.

- **Extinct In The Wild** Known only to survive in captivity, or as a population that has been reintroduced.

- **Extinct** Species that no longer exist.

# The animal kingdom

Our planet is inhabited by many kinds of creatures. This diagram shows the classification of animals based on their features. Inside the book you'll find animals from all of these groups.

**Birds**
Feathers make these vertebrates unique.

**Amphibians**
These vertebrates live partly in water and partly on land.

**Reptiles**
These cold-blooded vertebrates have scaly skin.

**Insects**
Insects are the most successful group of invertebrates.

**Fish**
Underwater vertebrates, fish breathe through gills.

**Vertebrates**
Animals with backbones are called vertebrates.

**Mammals**
These warm-blooded, furry vertebrates feed their young on milk.

**Invertebrates**
These animals have no backbones.

**Animals**
They are the largest group of living things, from aardvarks to zebras.

# The quiz starts here ...

# Powerful predator

What **animal** is this?

Does it **hunt** alone?

What helps it **hide** in long grass?

What does it **eat**?

Is it **endangered**?

Why does it have cushioned **pads** on its feet?

**Mammals**
*Panthera tigris*

# Tiger

The largest of the big cats, the tiger is one of the most powerful predators on Earth. Relying on its enormous strength, it is adapted to hunting big prey. Few predators regularly hunt alone for animals larger than themselves, but a tiger may take on a buffalo six times its own weight.

**Location** Asia

**Habitat** 🌳 🌲 🌴 ⛰️

**Diet** Mainly large, hoofed mammals

**Status** Endangered

**Length** 4½–9¼ ft (1.4–2.8 m)

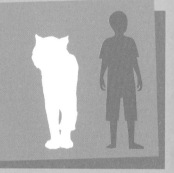

Each tiger has its own unique stripe pattern. No two tigers are alike, just like human fingerprints. These unique markings are useful for those identifying different tigers in the wild.

A tiger's feet have cushioned pads for stealthy hunting.

The tiger's dark stripes act as very effective camouflage, especially among long grass, where they mimic the vertical pattern of light and shade.

# King of the beasts

What **animal** is this?

What is its natural **habitat**?

Does it have any natural **predators**?

Where in the **world** does it live?

What is the name for a **group** of this animal?

Where does it usually **sleep**?

# Lion

More than 10,000 years ago, lions roamed the whole of Europe, Asia, and Africa. Apart from a small number in northwest India, lions today are found only in Africa. They are often seen napping under trees. Since they have no natural predators, they are perfectly safe sleeping in the open.

**Location** Africa, Asia

**Habitat**

**Diet** Large animals, such as zebras

**Status** Vulnerable

**Length** 5¼–8¼ft (1.6–2.5m)

A lion pride varies in size according to location and the availability of prey. The adult females and their young outnumber the adult males.

A lion's mane darkens with age.

The lionesses are the core of any pride, and stick close to their female relatives. They have strong, lithe bodies and creep stealthily before moving in for the kill.

What **animal** is this?

Is it **endangered**?

What does it **eat**?

What is this animal's natural **habitat**?

Is it a **social** creature?

How does it hunt down its **prey**?

**Mammals**
*Panthera uncia*

# Snow leopard

People in the Himalayan mountains often call the snow leopard the "ghost of the mountains." Little is known about these shy and solitary animals, which live high up in the icy mountains of Asia. These cats are rarely spotted by humans, as they live in isolated areas, among the world's highest peaks.

**Location** Asia

**Habitat** ▲▲

**Diet** Small prey, such as hares

**Status** Vulnerable

**Length** 2¾–4¼ft (0.9–1.25m)

As well as for balance, a snow leopard uses its furry tail to keep warm.

Snow leopards have their babies in the spring. The cubs stay with their mother through their first winter, before finding homes of their own.

The snow leopard's extra-long, bushy tail helps it keep its balance when leaping from rock to rock in pursuit of prey. It often chases animals down steep slopes, rarely losing its footing.

What **animal** is this?

What are its **markings** called?

Where does it **live**?

Can it **swim**?

What does this animal **eat**?

Does it have retractable **claws**?

How does it use its **paws** when hunting?

# Jaguar

The third largest of all the big cats, the jaguar lives in areas of Central and South America. Found in swampy grasslands and dense tropical rainforests, it lives and hunts in the water as well as on the ground. Fish are part of their main diet—jaguars simply flip them out of the water with their huge paws.

**Location** Central America, South America

**Habitat**

**Diet** Small mammals, fish, reptiles

**Status** Near Threatened

**Length** 4–5½ ft (1.2–1.7 m)

Jaguars often spend time swimming. They are never far from the water and regularly patrol the riverbanks looking for food.

A jaguar's retractable claws always stay sharp.

The jaguar's markings are called rosettes. They have a dark marking at the center.

# Speedy sprinter

What **animal** is this?

What is its natural **habitat**?

How **fast** can it run?

Where in the **world** does it live?

Why are its **canine teeth** smaller than other big cats'?

How can prey **dodge** this predator?

**Mammals**
*Acinonyx jubatus*

# Cheetah

Renowned as the world's fastest land animal, the cheetah can sprint at more than 62 mph (100 kph). This cat is uniquely adapted for accelerating faster than most sports cars, and pursuing its prey over short distances at blistering speed. Only the swiftest, most agile of its prey can hope to escape.

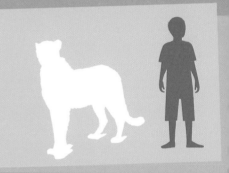

**Location** Africa, Asia

**Habitat** 🌵 🌿

**Diet** Small grazing animals

**Status** Vulnerable

**Length** 3½–5ft (1.1–1.5m)

A cheetah can only run at top speed for 10–20 seconds.

Compared with typical big cats, the cheetah has small canine teeth. The nostrils take up a lot of space in its skull, leaving no room for broad upper-canine tooth roots.

Cheetahs usually hunt small prey—to escape they must be agile enough to quickly change direction.

# Ocean hunter

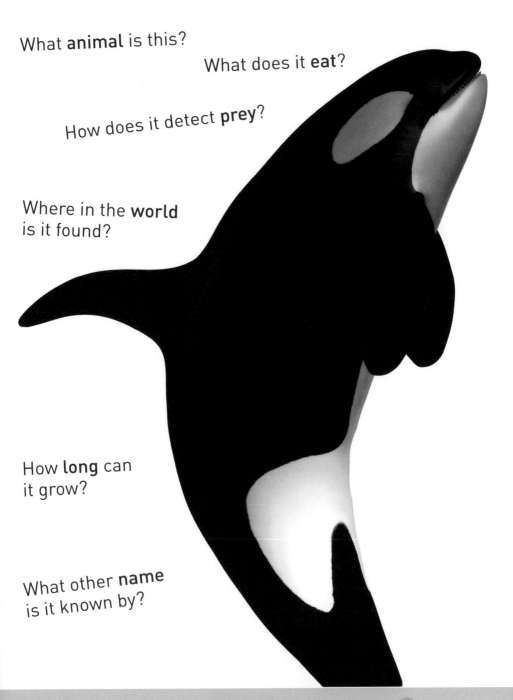

What **animal** is this?

What does it **eat**?

How does it detect **prey**?

Where in the **world** is it found?

How **long** can it grow?

What other **name** is it known by?

**Mammals**
*Orcinus orca*

# Killer whale

Distinctive black-and-white markings make the killer whale, also called orca, the most easily recognized of the toothed whales and dolphins. Like other members of the dolphin family, it has a taste for fish. However, it hunts big marine mammals, too, and regularly comes close to the shoreline on the trail of seals.

**Location** Worldwide

**Habitat**

**Diet** Fish, seals, other cetaceans

**Status** Data Deficient

**Length** Up to 32¼ ft (9.8 m)

The killer whale's dorsal fin and paddle-like flippers provide stability. The dorsal fin in males is taller and less curved than in females.

A killer whale detects prey using echolocation.

Killer whales travel together in groups called pods, which can consist of more than 50 individuals.

# Sociable seagoers

What **animal** is this?

What is a **group** of this animal called?

What is this animal's natural **habitat**?

How many **teeth** does it have?

What does it **eat**?

How does it **communicate** when traveling in groups?

Does it **sleep**?

**Mammals**
*Tursiops truncatus*

# Bottlenose dolphin

Fast, agile, and intelligent, bottlenose dolphins are ruthlessly efficient hunters of fish and squid. They are small, toothed whales, so highly specialized for life at sea that they can outswim most fish. They travel across oceans in groups called pods, staying in touch using a variety of sounds.

**Location** Worldwide (except polar regions)

**Habitat**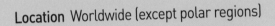

**Diet** Fish, mollusks, crustaceans

**Status** Least Concern

**Length** 6¼–13ft (1.9–4m)

The dolphin's big, curved mouth makes it look like it's smiling. It grips fish with 80–100 small, sharp teeth.

A dolphin sleeps by resting half of its brain at a time.

Dolphins are always on the move—they love to chase each other and ride the waves.

# Gentle giant

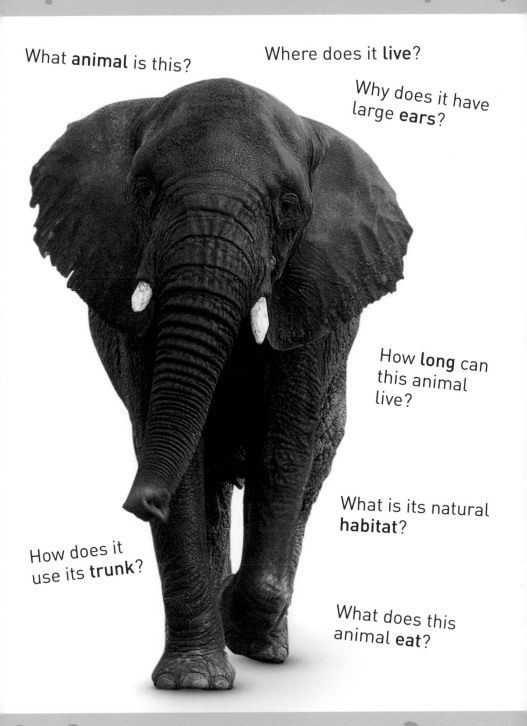

What **animal** is this?

Where does it **live**?

Why does it have large **ears**?

How **long** can this animal live?

What is its natural **habitat**?

How does it use its **trunk**?

What does this animal **eat**?

**Mammals**
*Loxodonta africana*

# African elephant

Elephants are the world's largest land animals. They live in close-knit family groups led by the oldest female. These animals have enormous pillar-like legs, large ears, and specialized incisor teeth in the form of tusks. African elephants are the largest of the three elephant species, and live for up to 70 years.

**Location** Africa

**Habitat**

**Diet** Bark, leaves, grass

**Status** Vulnerable

**Length** 13–16ft (4–5m)

The elephant's trunk makes an ideal tool for investigating and gathering food, drawing in water, and signaling to other elephants.

An elephant's large ears radiate heat to prevent overheating.

# Fierce hunter

What **animal** is this?

How did it get its **name**?

Where does it **live**?

How can it eat **venomous** snakes?

How does it mark its **territory**?

**Mammals**
*Mellivora capensis*

# Honey badger

Renowned for its ferocity when backed into a tight corner, the honey badger is prepared to eat almost any animal it can catch, including highly venomous snakes. It is thought that the honey badger has some immunity to a snake's venom, which allows it to attack and eat a cobra without risking a fatal bite.

**Location** Africa, Asia

**Habitat** 

**Diet** Animals, fruit, honey

**Status** Least Concern

**Length** 29–38 in (73–96 cm)

Although mainly a carnivore, the honey badger owes its name to its taste for honeycomb, which it rips from bees' nests without regard for their stings.

A honey badger marks its territory with smelly liquid.

What **animal** is this?

Where in the **world** does it live?

When is it most **active**?

What helps this animal **cool** down?

What does it **eat**?

Is it a fast or slow **runner**?

**Mammals**
*Lepus californicus*

# Black-tailed jackrabbit

The enormous ears of the jackrabbit are vital to its survival in hot, dry deserts and grasslands, because they act as radiators that give off excess heat to the air and help the animal keep cool. Despite its name, the jackrabbit is a hare, with long legs that give it the speed to escape a coyote.

**Location** US, Mexico

**Habitat**

**Diet** Grass, herbs, twigs

**Status** Least Concern

**Length** 20½–24 in (52–61 cm)

Black-tailed jackrabbits are widespread in semiarid regions. They avoid heat by being active mostly at night. Unusually for hares, they occasionally burrow to escape excessive heat.

Baby hares, called leverets, are born fully furred and open-eyed.

# Snowy hopper

What **animal** is this?

What is its natural **habitat**?

How does it **camouflage** itself in changing conditions?

Does it live **alone**?

Where in the **world** does it live?

Is it **endangered**?

How far can it **leap**?

**Mammals**
*Lepus arcticus*

# Arctic hare

The Arctic hare lives in the treeless tundra habitat found near the North Pole. A true survivor, it can endure the long and bitter winter. Preferred sites are rocky outcrops or hillsides with crevices and crannies for shelter. This hare may be solitary but, especially in winter, large groups of up to 300 gather together.

**Location** Canada, Greenland

**Habitat**

**Diet** Grasses, herbs, shrubs

**Status** Least Concern

**Length** 22–26 in (56–66 cm)

Male hares stand up on their hind legs to box each other in the fight for mates.

The Arctic hare can travel 6 ft (2 m) in a single leap.

The Arctic hare's coat changes color with the passing seasons—a white coat is the perfect camouflage in snowy surroundings, and it can turn gray or brown if the snow melts.

# Majestic antlers

What **animal** is this?

Where in the **world** does it live?

Is it **endangered**?

How often does a male grow new **antlers**?

How do its wide **hooves** help it move around?

**Mammals**
*Alces alces*

31

# Moose

Moose are the largest deer, with males up to twice as heavy as females. They like wet places and live in forests, wetlands, and near lakes, where they can feast on aquatic plants. Only males have antlers, which they use to fight for females. Antlers fall off in the fall and grow in spring.

**Location** Alaska, Canada, Europe, Asia

**Habitat** 🌳 🌲 🌾 〰️

**Diet** Leaves, moss, bark, water plants

**Status** Least Concern

**Length** 7¾– 9¾ ft (2.4–3 m)

The antlers are up to 6½ ft (2 m) in length.

The moose's wide hooves help it walk on soft snow and wade through muddy lakes and swamps.

Male moose grow a new set of antlers every spring. These have a velvet covering, which is shed in the fall—the mating season.

# Santa's helper

What **animal** is this?

What is this animal's natural **habitat**?

Where in the **world** does it live?

Do both males and females grow **antlers**?

How do its **hooves** change during the year?

How far can it **migrate**?

What does it **eat**?

**Mammals**
*Rangifer tarandus*

# Reindeer

Also known as caribou in North America, reindeer are well adapted to life in the Arctic tundra. They have a dense coat and broad, flat hooves, which provide stability on soft summer ground and act as snowshoes in winter, when they become harder and sharper-edged—ideal for cutting through snow and ice.

**Location** North America, Greenland, Europe, Asia

**Habitat** 🌲🌲🌲 ⛰️ 🏔️

**Diet** Leaves, roots, bark, lichen

**Status** Vulnerable

**Length** 5¾–6¾ ft (1.7–2.1 m)

Female reindeer are the only female deer that have antlers.

Reindeer can migrate 3,000 miles (5,000 km) in a year—the longest distance any land mammal travels.

American reindeer (shown here) have mainly brown coats. European and Asian reindeer are more gray.

34

# Two humps

What **animal** is this?

How long can it go without **water**?

Is it **endangered**?

What does it **eat**?

What is this animal's natural **habitat**?

What is special about its **nostrils**?

How much **water** can it drink in 10 minutes?

**Mammals**
*Camelus ferus*

# Wild bactrian camel

The wild bactrian camel is two-humped and can tolerate extreme heat. After a drought, it can drink 24 gallons (110 liters) of water in 10 minutes. They are well suited to the desert because they can go for days without water. Their body temperature can rise several degrees before they need to sweat.

**Location** Asia

**Habitat**

**Diet** Grass, leaves, shrubs

**Status** Critically Endangered

**Length** 10¼–11¼ft (3.2–3.5m)

Bactrian camels have long, shaggy fur that covers the upper surface of the foot.

A camel can close its nostrils to seal them against dust.

Fewer than a thousand wild bactrian camels still survive in the Gobi Desert in Asia. They have thick fur to keep them warm during the cold winters.

What **animal** is this?

Where in the **world** does this animal live?

What are the names of its domestic **descendants**?

What does it **eat**?

Is it a **social** or **solitary** creature?

What are its **babies** called?

What is special about its **blood**?

# Guanaco

Guanacos live in herds and prefer cold, mountainous habitats, including grassland and forest. Their blood has a very high concentration of oxygen-carrying red blood cells that enables them to live in thin, high-altitude air. They can also survive in deserts, including the Atacama—the driest hot desert on Earth.

**Location** South America

**Habitat**

**Diet** Grass, shrubs, fungi

**Status** Least Concern

**Length** 3–7 ft (0.9–2.1 m)

The guanaco is found wild in South America. Their domestic descendants, the llama and alpaca, have been bred in the Andes since the time of the Inca civilization.

A baby guanaco is known as a chulengo.

Guanacos live in herds made up of a dominant male, females, and infants.

# Ship of the desert

What **animal** is this?

What does it **eat**?

How long ago was this animal **domesticated**?

What is this animal's natural **habitat**?

What is the name for the way it **walks**?

How does it stay **cool**?

How do its feet stop it **sinking** into sand?

**Mammals**
*Camelus dromedarius*

# Dromedary

The Arabian dromedary was domesticated at least 4,000 years ago, and is now considered extinct in the wild throughout its native range. The dromedary can go for days without water in temperatures that would give other mammals fatal heatstroke, and can eat almost any vegetation it finds.

**Location** Africa, Asia

**Habitat**

**Diet** Leaves, grasses

**Status** Not Evaluated

**Length** 7¼–11 ft (2.2–3.4 m)

A dromedary has thick fur to keep its skin cool.

The broad, two-toed feet of the dromedary are well-adapted to walking across wind-blown dunes. They spread under the dromedary's weight to stop them sinking into the soft sand.

Camels move their front and back legs on the same side forward together in a rocking motion. This distinctive gait is known as pacing.

# Ringed horns

What **animal** is this?

How is the **coloring** different for males and females?

Do males or females have larger **horns**?

What is its **endangered** status?

Where does this animal **live**?

What does this animal **eat**?

# Sable antelope

The male southern sable antelope is black, except for its cheeks, chin, and underparts. Females are smaller and browner, but both sexes have heavily ringed horns that curve up and back from the forehead. In the rainy season, males compete for territories, and the victors dominate small herds of females.

**Location** Africa

**Habitat**

**Diet** Grass, leaves

**Status** Least Concern

**Length** 6¼–8¾ft (1.9–2.7m)

Infant males have chestnut colored fur on their body. As they grow older, the fur turns black. Females have chestnut to dark-brown fur all their lives.

The horns of a male sable antelope are nearly 3 ft (1m) long.

Mature males are black, but with the same facial pattern as females. They have larger, more curved horns than females.

# Majestic giant

What **animal** is this?

What does this animal **eat**?

What is its natural **habitat**?

How **fast** can it move?

How does its long **tongue** help it?

How does it **drink**?

How many bones does it have in its **neck**?

**Mammals**
*Giraffa camelopardalis*

# Northern giraffe

The majestic giraffe is the tallest of all living animals. Much of the giraffe's height comes from its elongated neck and legs. It has thick blood vessels, high blood pressure, and a powerful heart to pump blood all the way to its brain. If alarmed, the giraffe can gallop at speeds of up to 35 mph (55 kph).

**Location** Africa

**Habitat** 🌿

**Diet** Tree leaves

**Status** Vulnerable

**Length** 9¾–15 ft (3.8–4.7 m)

The giraffe's great height means that to drink water it must spread its front legs wide, and even bend at the knees.

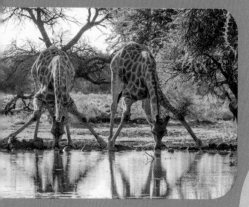

The giraffe often feeds on tall acacia trees. But acacia twigs are thorny, so it uses its long tongue to probe between the thorns and pull out the leaves.

The giraffe's neck is made of the same seven bones found in humans—but each bone is much longer.

# Rock climber

What **animal** is this?

Can the **babies** climb shortly after they are born?

What is its natural **habitat**?

How does its thick **fur** help it?

What does it **eat**?

Does it have a **beard**?

**Mammals**
*Oreamnos americanus*

# Mountain goat

Many mountain mammals have thick fur to protect them from the icy weather. The mountain goat looks like it has a beard like other goats, but it is actually just an extension of its throat mane. The mountain goat is an expert rock climber, and baby goats (kids) can walk and climb shortly after they are born.

**Location** North America

**Habitat**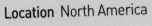

**Diet** Grass, twigs

**Status** Least Concern

**Length** 4½–5¾ ft (1.4–1.8 m)

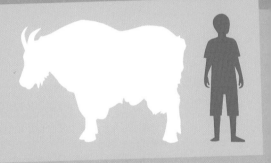

Mountain goat hooves have soles that provide grip on rocky surfaces.

A baby goat can stand minutes after birth, and follows its mother over steep slopes within days.

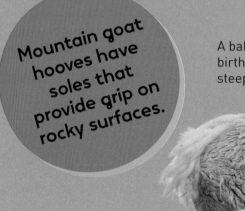

# Sleek hunter

What **animal** is this?

Where does this animal **live**?

How does it stay **warm** in cold water?

How do its **whiskers** help it?

What does it **eat**?

Where does it give **birth** to its babies?

**Mammals**
*Phoca vitulina*

# Common seal

Seals are warm-blooded animals, which means they maintain a constant body temperature. Because they often swim in cold water, they need to retain their body heat. They are covered in dense fur and have a layer of fat, called blubber. In warmer waters seals often fan their flippers in the air to cool down.

**Location** North Atlantic, North Pacific

**Habitat**

**Diet** Fish, shellfish

**Status** Least Concern

**Length** 4–6¼ ft (1.2–1.9 m)

This seal's blubber layer is about 8 cm (3 in) thick.

Baby seals, or pups, are born on land. For a few weeks, many of them have white, fluffy fur.

The seal's whiskers, which are 40 times thicker than human hair, can sense movement in the water. This helps the seal find food to eat, such as shellfish.

# Magnificent tusks

What **animal** is this?

Where in the **world** does it live?

What is special about its **nostrils**?

How does it keep its **head** above water?

How does it find food in **murky** water?

What is its main **diet**?

What is this animal **renowned** for?

# Walrus

Renowned for its magnificent tusks, the walrus is a big, thick-skinned relative of seals and sea lions. It hunts in shallow seas, diving to the seabed beneath the pack ice to find its prey. Walruses feed mainly on clams, which they locate in dark, murky water by feeling for them with their highly sensitive whiskers.

**Location** Arctic waters

**Habitat**

**Diet** Seabed animals

**Status** Data Deficient

**Length** 8¼–11¼ft (2.5–3.5m)

When a walrus dives underwater, its nostrils close automatically to keep the water out.

A walrus has a big air sac in its throat that it can inflate to keep its head above water. It may even sleep like this. Males also use the air sac to add resonance to their calls when competing with rivals or displaying to females.

# Master of grasses

What **animal** is this?

Where in the **world** does this animal live?

Is it **endangered**?

What is its natural **habitat**?

How does it **cool** off?

Does it live in **herds**?

What animal does it **run** like?

What animal does it **swim** like?

**Mammals**
*Hydrochoerus hydrochaeris*

# Capybara

South American swamps are home to a rodent the size of a pig. The capybara, which means "master of grasses" in the local language, is a social animal that lives in herds. On land it runs like a horse, and in water it swims like a beaver. When grazing, the capybara uses its front incisor teeth to crop grass.

**Location** South America

**Habitat** 〰〰

**Diet** Grasses, plants

**Status** Least Concern

**Length** 3½–4½ft (1.1–1.3m)

Capybaras are the biggest rodents on Earth.

On a hot afternoon, capybaras cool off in rivers and lakes. They laze around in the water for hours with their family members. In the evening, they go to find food.

The capybara is heavy bodied, with short but sturdy limbs. Its nostrils, eyes, and ears are set on top of its head, so it can smell, see, and hear when swimming.

# Speedy swimmer

What **animal** is this?

Where in the **world** does it live?

How **long** can it grow?

Does it like to **swim** out to sea?

How long can it hold its **breath**?

Does it always lie **flat**?

How deep can it **dive**?

# California sea lion

California sea lions are sociable and live in noisy, crowded groups called colonies, near rocky ocean shores—they rarely stray far out to sea. These intelligent, highly efficient hunters of fast-swimming fish and squid can dive to depths of 100 ft (30 m) or more, holding their breath for up to ten minutes.

**Location** US

**Habitat**

**Diet** Fish, squid

**Status** Least Concern

**Length** Up to 7½ ft (2.4 m)

A sea lion breathes out before diving.

In the breeding season, male sea lions fight each other fiercely for females. The largest males are the most successful in these conflicts.

Unlike a seal, which always lies flat on land, a sea lion can prop itself up on its front flippers. It can also turn its hind flippers forward to walk on all fours.

What **animal** is this?

What is this animal's natural **habitat**?

How long does a **baby** stay with its mother?

Where does this animal **sleep**?

How does the **face** of a male look different from a female?

What is its **endangered** status?

What does it **eat**?

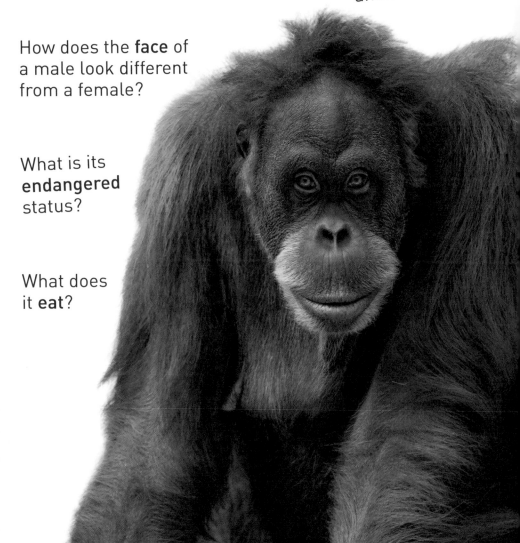

**Mammals**
*Pongo pygmaeus*

# Bornean orangutan

The orangutan is very much a tree-dwelling animal, feeding, sleeping, and breeding in the forest canopy, with only males occasionally coming to the ground. It spends most of the day looking for and eating fruit and other food, and at night it builds a sleeping platform by weaving branches together.

**Location** Asia

**Habitat**

**Diet** Fruit, plants, honey, small animals

**Status** Critically Endangered

**Length** 28–38 in (72–97 cm)

The male orangutan looks strikingly different from the female, with large cheek pads, which grow bigger as the animal ages.

The female gives birth in a treetop nest, and the tiny infant clings to its mother as she clambers about the canopy. The pair will stay together until the youngster is about eight years old.

Orangutan means "person of the forest."

What **animal** is this?

Is it **endangered**?

Where in the **world** does it live?

Is it **intelligent**?

Is it a **social** or **solitary** creature?

When does it look for **food**?

**Mammals**
*Gorilla gorilla*

# Western gorilla

The mighty Western gorilla is the biggest of the apes—a forest giant that is one of our closest living relatives. It is highly intelligent and lives in small, stable family groups of 3–20. Each group is defended by a single mature "silverback" male, who uses his prodigious strength to keep rival males at bay.

**Location** Africa

**Habitat**

**Diet** Leaves, bark, fruit

**Status** Critically Endangered

**Length** 3¼–3½ft (1–1.1m)

The newborn gorilla will cling to its mother's fur for around five months. After that, the youngster will ride on its mother's back or shoulders.

Gorillas spend their mornings and evenings looking for food and eating, and the middle part of the day sleeping, playing, or grooming.

A gorilla only stands to fight or beat its chest.

# Super intelligent

What **animal** is this?

Why are **numbers** of this animal low?

Where in the **world** does it live?

What does it **eat**?

What does it use as **tools**?

Where does it **sleep**?

**Mammals**
*Pan troglodytes*

# Common chimpanzee

Chimpanzees live in communities of about 35 members, although exceptionally large groups may have up to 150. Active by day, they spend half of it foraging in the forest for plants and animals. Some groups are known to eat as many as 200 types of food. Each evening, they construct sleeping nests in the treetops.

**Location** Africa

**Habitat**

**Diet** Plants, animals

**Status** Endangered

**Length** 28–38in (70–96cm)

Chimpanzees were once spread throughout the tropical forests of West and Central Africa. Today their numbers are low due to many factors, including deforestation and capture by humans.

Young chimps are inquisitive and playful, enjoying games of rough and tumble with their playmates.

Chimpanzees are very intelligent— they have learned how to use sticks and stones as tools.

# Island acrobat

What **animal** is this?

Is it **endangered**?

Does it only live in the **trees**?

What does it **eat**?

Where in the **world** does it live?

Is it a **solitary** animal?

**Mammals**
*Lemur catta*

# Ring-tailed lemur

Found only in Madagascar, the lemurs are a diverse group of primates related to the ancestors of monkeys and apes. They are highly adapted to life in the forest, and many are superbly acrobatic climbers. The ring-tailed lemur's distinctive tail makes it the most recognizable of the lemurs.

**Location** Madagascar

**Habitat**

**Diet** Fruit, leaves, small animals

**Status** Endangered

**Length** 15¼–18in (39–46cm)

The female ring-tailed lemurs are always in charge.

The ring-tailed lemur enjoys basking in sunshine, whether on the ground or in trees. It often sits with hands on knees.

Ring-tailed lemurs live in large, noisy groups, searching for fruit, leaves, and small animals in the forest. Unusually for lemurs, they also spend a lot of time on the ground.

# American powerhouse

What **animal** is this?

Do **males** and **females** live together?

Where in the **world** does it live?

What is another name for a **male**?

What does it **eat**?

How does it **spend** most of its day?

What caused its numbers to drop **dramatically**?

# American bison

Sometimes called American buffalo, these huge animals roam in groups, spending the greater part of their day grazing. The females form herds with their calves under the leadership of a dominant female. The males, or bulls, live in separate herds and usually approach the cows only in the mating season.

**Location** North America

**Habitat**

**Diet** Grass, sedges

**Status** Near Threatened

**Length** 7–11 ft (2.1–3.5 m)

With its massively thick coat and shaggy mane, the American bison stays warm even when the temperature drops below freezing.

An adult American bison could leap over an adult human.

Excessive hunting in earlier centuries wiped out millions of American bison. The remaining herds live mainly in protected areas.

# Tireless trekkers

What **animal** is this?

What is this animal's natural **habitat**?

When migrating in herds, they get **ambushed** by hippos. True or false?

What does its baby **sound** like?

What is its **diet**?

What color is its **coat**?

**Mammals**
*Connochaetes taurinus*

# Blue wildebeest

The blue wildebeest has a silver-gray coat, and the tail is long and black. It has an unmistakable large, long muzzled head, cowlike horns, and high shoulders. A single calf is born after eight to nine months' gestation. It bleats like a lamb, and its fiercely protective mother bellows like a domestic cow in reply.

**Location** Africa

**Habitat**

**Diet** Grass

**Status** Least Concern

**Length** 5–7¾ ft (1.5–2.4 m)

Every year, more than 1 million wildebeest trek across the Serengeti.

Herds of wildebeest migrate across the Serengeti plains during the dry season in search of food and water. They have to cross the Mara River, where Nile crocodiles lie in wait to ambush them.

# Jumping antelope

What **animal** is this?

Where does it **live**?

What is its **endangered** status?

Why does it **leap**?

What is the name for its **leaping** habit?

It has a four-chambered **stomach** for processing fibrous food. True or false?

**Mammals**
*Antidorcas marsupialis*

# Cape springbok

The highly agile Cape springbok gets its name from its habit of "pronking"—leaping stiff-legged, high, and repeatedly off the ground, as if bouncing. This behavior may serve as a warning to other springbok, and to demonstrate fitness, encouraging any predators to pick on a weaker victim.

**Location** Africa

**Habitat** 🌱

**Diet** Grass, leaves

**Status** Least Concern

**Length** 4–4½ft (1.2–1.4m)

Pronking is mainly carried out by the young, often in response to danger.

Springbok means "jumping antelope" in Afrikaans.

Springboks have four-chambered stomachs for processing bulky, fibrous food such as grass.

What **animal** is this?

What is its natural **habitat**?

Is it a **social** creature?

Does it live **above** ground?

What is its **diet**?

What does it use its long **claws** for?

**Mammals**
*Suricata suricatta*

# Meerkat

The meerkat's habit of standing up on its hind legs, either to watch for predators or bask in the morning sun, has made this slender desert mongoose one of the most instantly recognizable of African mammals. The meerkat is sociable, living in clans of around 20 in large networks of underground burrows.

**Location** Africa

**Habitat**

**Diet** Insects, small animals

**Status** Least Concern

**Length** 9¼–11½ in (25–29 cm)

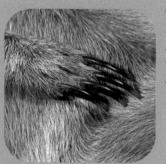

The long claws on the meerkat's front paws are adapted for digging to make burrows and to find food.

A meerkat pup is so tiny, it can fit in the palm of your hand.

Each meerkat clan is dominated by one breeding pair that produces most of the young. Other adults in the clan help care for the pups.

# Pack animal

What **animal** is this?

What does it **eat**?

Where does this animal **live**?

Is it **endangered**?

Can it live **alone**?

How **fast** can it run?

How does it **hunt** its prey?

How does the color of its coat help it get **close** to its prey?

**Mammals**
*Lycaon pictus*

# African wild dog

The African wild dog is one of the most social carnivores and cannot survive on its own. Its life revolves around the pack— an extended family of up to 30 adults and young that live and hunt together in the woodlands and broad, grassy plains of Africa. It relies on the strength of the pack to pull prey to the ground.

**Location** Africa

**Habitat** ⛰️ 🌾 🏞️

**Diet** Large mammals

**Status** Critically Endangered

**Length** 30–43 in (76–141 cm)

African wild dogs can run at speeds of more than 30 mph (50 kph).

Lean, lightweight, and long-legged, the African wild dog has incredible stamina and hunts by chasing prey to exhaustion.

The African wild dog's random blotches of black, tan, yellow, and white provide camouflage in forests, scrub, and tall grass, allowing them to get close to their prey.

# Champion howler

What **animal** is this?

What does it **eat**?

What is this animal's natural **habitat**?

How does it **track** its prey?

How many **pups** can the dominant female have?

When do **pups** emerge from the den?

Does it **hunt** alone?

**Mammals**
*Canis lupus*

73

# Gray wolf

The ancestor of all domestic dogs, the gray wolf was once common throughout all northern continents. Now, its howl is rarely heard outside the remote regions of the far north and a few mountain refuges. Wolves prey mainly on other mammals, but are rarely strong enough to tackle large prey alone.

**Location** North America, Europe, Asia

**Habitat** 🌳 🌲 ⛰ ⌂

**Diet** Large mammals

**Status** Least Concern

**Length** 3–4¼ft (0.9–1.3m)

The dominant female gives birth to between 1 and 11 pups. After a month, pups emerge from the den to receive scraps of food.

A gray wolf's howl can be heard by other pack members up to 7 miles (11km) away.

The gray wolf's long snout gives it an acute sense of smell. Wolves rely heavily on scents for both tracking their prey and communicating with each other.

What **animal** is this?

What is this animal's natural **habitat**?

Is it **endangered**?

What does it **eat**?

Does it live **alone**?

How does its coat **change** during the year?

It can withstand **temperatures** of -94°F (-70°C). True or false?

Which part of it isn't **furry**?

**Mammals**
*Alopex lagopus*

# Arctic fox

Able to withstand extreme polar temperatures of -94°F (-70°C), the Arctic fox keeps warm with a fluffy, double-layered coat of winter fur. Its coat is almost pure white in winter for camouflage in snow and ice. Most Arctic foxes turn gray in summer, though some stay gray all year round.

**Location** Canada, Alaska, Greenland, Europe, Asia

**Habitat**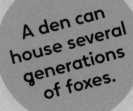

**Diet** Lemmings, birds, eggs, fish, fruit

**Status** Least Concern

**Length** 20–30in (50–75cm)

The Arctic fox has small ears, short legs, and a short tail, since these areas lose heat fastest. Every part of its body except its nose is thickly furred.

A den can house several generations of foxes.

The Arctic fox's dark summer coat is half as thick as its winter one, with less than half of the underfur.

# Masked bandit

What **animal** is this?

When is it **active**?

Where in the **world** does it live?

Where does it normally make its **den**?

Is it a **social** creature?

When does it **hunt**?

How can it **open** doors?

**Mammals**
*Procyon lotor*

# Northern raccoon

Active day and night, and normally solitary, northern raccoons may gather in groups to find food sources, such as garbage dumpsters. Raccoons are not picky in their choice of food and will eat almost anything. They use their front paws, which are highly sensitive to touch, to examine their food before eating it.

**Location** The Americas

**Habitat**

**Diet** Fruit, small mammals, insects

**Status** Least Concern

**Length** 17½–24 in (44–62 cm)

**The five toes on a raccoon's forepaws function like human fingers.**

Raccoons generally make their dens in hollow trees or burrows, where they hole up during the day. They emerge to hunt at dusk.

The bandit-like appearance suits the raccoon's behavior. A frequent visitor to urban areas, it can use its forepaws to manipulate doors and latches.

What **animal** is this?

What is its main **diet**?

Where in the **world** does it live?

Can it **swim**?

Does it avoid **humans**?

How does it **escape** predators?

**Mammals**
*Didelphis virginiana*

# Virginia opossum

The highly adaptable Virginia opossum is the largest American marsupial. It benefits from human habitation, both for shelter, because it nests in piles of debris or buildings, and for food, because it scavenges for scraps. The Virginia opossum usually stays on the ground, but also climbs well and swims strongly.

**Location** US, Mexico, Central America

**Habitat**

**Diet** Fruits, insects, carrion

**Status** Least Concern

**Length** 13–20 in (33–50 cm)

The Virginia opossum plays dead to trick predators, lying on one side with its eyes and mouth open. Most predators eat live prey so they leave the "dead" opossum alone.

The Virginia opossum is common in many US cities.

# Nocturnal devil

What **animal** is this?

What is the **largest** prey it can catch?

What is its natural **habitat**?

Is it **endangered**?

Why does it have a **white** chest patch?

Where in the **world** does this animal live?

**Mammals**
*Sarcophilus harrisii*

# Tasmanian devil

The largest marsupial carnivore, the nocturnal Tasmanian devil hunts prey of varied sizes and also scavenges. Most Tasmanian devils are not aggressive unless threatened or competing with another devil for food. When more than one animal is drawn to the same carcass, a noisy squabble might develop.

**Location** Tasmania

**Habitat**

**Diet** Carrion, living animals, plants

**Status** Endangered

**Length** 22½–26¼ in (57–66 cm)

A Tasmanian devil can take prey up to the size of a small kangaroo.

The white chest patch of a Tasmanian devil is particularly distinctive. The patch may act as a flag to draw aggressive bites from other devils away from the more vulnerable face.

# Picky eater

What **animal** is this?

Where does it **live**?

What does it **eat**?

What is this animal's **endangered** status?

What is the **first** thing a baby eats?

How **long** does it sleep every day?

**Mammals**
*Phascolarctos cinereus*

# Koala

Koalas have evolved the ability to eat a plant that would poison most other animals—eucalyptus. They are picky eaters, however, feeding only on a few of the 600-plus eucalyptus species found in Australia. They also avoid eating leaves from trees growing in poor soil because these are the most toxic.

**Location** Australia

**Habitat**

**Diet** Eucalyptus leaves

**Status** Vulnerable

**Length** 26–32 in (65–82 cm)

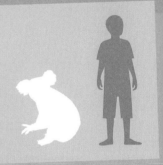

Eucalyptus leaves provide little energy, so koalas sleep up to 18 hours a day, and take rests between bouts of feeding.

Koalas eat such large quantities of eucalyptus leaves that their body oil smells like cough drops.

A young koala clings to its mother. Its first meal is its mother's specialized form of droppings called pap, which carry microbes to help it digest eucalyptus leaves.

# Speedy hopper

What **animal** is this?

Where does this animal **live**?

What is its **young** called?

What is its **diet**?

How does a mother **carry** its young?

What does it use its **paws** for?

How **fast** can it travel?

# Red kangaroo

The biggest Australian mammal, and the largest of all marsupials, the red kangaroo is a spectacularly agile creature adapted for life on dry grassland. Its powerful hind legs enable it to hop across the open landscape at high speed with minimal effort. The red kangaroo can reach 30 mph (50 kph) for short periods.

**Location** Australia

**Habitat**

**Diet** Mostly grass

**Status** Least Concern

**Length** 2¼–4½ft (0.7–1.4m)

The forelimbs end in dexterous paws that are used for feeding, grooming, self-defense.

A red kangaroo is as tall as a human, but at birth, it is just ¾in (2 cm) long.

A female may carry a young "joey" in her pouch until it is at least seven months old.

# Bushy-tailed rodent

What **animal** is this?

Does it **hibernate**?

Where in the **world** does it live?

How can it get **seeds** out of cones?

What does it do for **most** of the day?

What are its **young** called?

How **far** can it leap?

**Mammals**
*Sciurus vulgaris*

# Eurasian red squirrel

Eurasian red squirrels spend most of the day feeding or collecting food, such as seeds and nuts. In the warmest hours of summer, they retire to a nest (drey). They do not hibernate, relying instead on their food stores to survive winter. Agile climbers, these rodents can leap distances of up to 13 ft (4 m).

**Location** Europe, Asia

**Habitat** 🌳 🌲 ⛰️

**Diet** Conifer seeds, nuts

**Status** Least Concern

**Length** 8–10 in (20–25 cm)

Eurasian red squirrels have remarkably varied coat colors, with the upper coats ranging from very light red to black.

When jumping from one tree to the next, the red squirrel uses its long tail to steer itself.

Squirrel kits spend their first weeks in a drey lined with soft moss and grass, opening their eyes at around five weeks old.

# Busy architect

What **animal** is this?

What is its natural **habitat**?

What is its **home** called?

Is it **endangered**?

How does it cut down **trees**?

What does it **eat**?

How long can it hold its **breath** underwater?

# American beaver

One of nature's busiest architects, the American beaver uses its tree-felling skills to transform the landscape of its native forests. It creates dams, lakes, and impenetrable fortresses where it is safe from its enemies. Its prominent, chisel-bladed front teeth are used for gnawing food and cutting down trees.

**Location** US

**Habitat** 〰〰

**Diet** Tree bark, leaves, twigs

**Status** Least Concern

**Length** 32–35in (80–90cm)

The American beaver needs trees to build its lodge, which it surrounds with a defensive moat of deep water by using timber and mud to dam a forest stream. When the water freezes over in winter, the beavers stay active beneath the ice. It feeds on the leaves and buds of branches stored underwater.

A beaver can hold its breath underwater for up to 15 minutes.

# Super soft fur

What **animal** is this?

What is its **endangered** status?

How does it stay **warm** at night?

Is it a **solitary** creature?

Why is it **hunted**?

How long is its **gestation** period?

Where in the **world** does it live?

**Mammals**
*Chinchilla lanigera*

# Chilean chinchilla

Prized for its soft, silky fur, the chinchilla has been hunted by humans for many years. It is named after a South American tribe called "Chincha," the members of which used to wear clothes made from the animal's fur. The chinchilla forms colonies of 100 or more in rocky areas, sheltering in caves and crevices.

**Location** South America

**Habitat** ⛰️

**Diet** Grass, leaves

**Status** Endangered

**Length** 8–9½ in (22–24 cm)

The Chilean chinchilla eats plant foods, especially grass and leaves, sitting up to hold items in its front feet while watching for danger.

Chinchillas have very thick fur—each of their hair follicles holds around 60 hairs.

Up to four young are born after a gestation period of about 16 weeks, and are suckled for 6 to 8 weeks.

# One tusk

What **animal** is this?

What is a family **group** of this animal called?

How does it catch **prey**?

What is its **tusk** used for?

Where in the **world** does this animal live?

What does it **eat**?

What is its natural **habitat**?

**Mammals**
*Monodon monoceros*

# Narwhal

Equipped with a long, spiral tusk rooted in its upper jaw, the spectacular narwhal is a marine predator specialized for hunting below Arctic pack ice. It is a species of whale and, in general, only the male has a tusk. The tusk is highly sensitive and may be used to sense temperature or the saltiness of the water.

**Location** Arctic Ocean

**Habitat**

**Diet** Fish, squid

**Status** Least Concern

**Length** 12–16¼ft (3.7–5m)

Males are thought to use their magnificent tusks to impress females. They may also be used for fighting or to show dominance.

The narwhal uses its powerful lips and tongue to suck prey into its mouth.

In winter, narwhals hunt in family groups called pods. The whales stay in contact using chirps, whistles, and squeaks, and rely on finding gaps in the ice where they can surface to breathe.

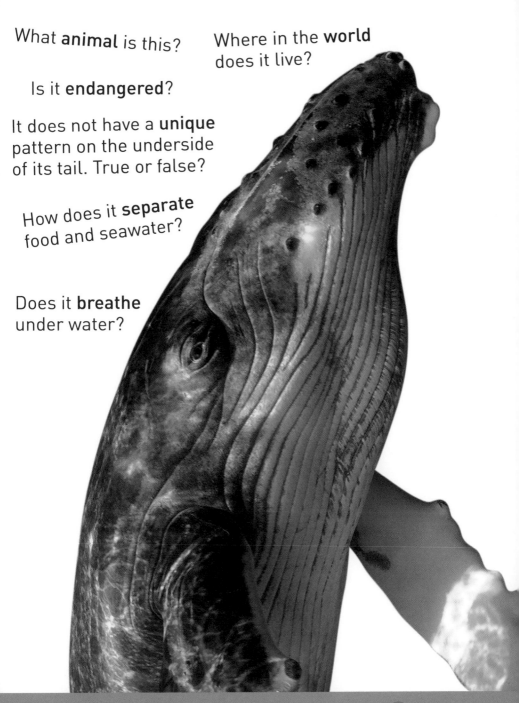

What **animal** is this?

Where in the **world** does it live?

Is it **endangered**?

It does not have a **unique** pattern on the underside of its tail. True or false?

How does it **separate** food and seawater?

Does it **breathe** under water?

**Mammals**
*Megaptera novaeangliae*

# Humpback whale

The humpback whale is one of the largest and heaviest living animals on the planet, and is renowned for its spectacular leaps right out of the water. It has a series of pleats beneath its mouth. When the whale is feeding, these pleats allow the throat to expand like a balloon and hold mouthfuls of fish and seawater.

**Location** Worldwide

**Habitat**

**Diet** Plankton, small fish

**Status** Least Concern

**Length** 49¼–55¾ ft (15–17 m)

Hundreds of bristles hang from the humpback whale's top jaw. The whale keeps its giant mouth open to gulp large amounts of fish, and sieves out the unwanted seawater using the thick mesh of bristles.

The pattern on the underside of every whale's tail is unique like a human fingerprint.

When the humpback whale surfaces to breathe, it blasts a spray of air and water through its blowholes high into the air before taking another breath.

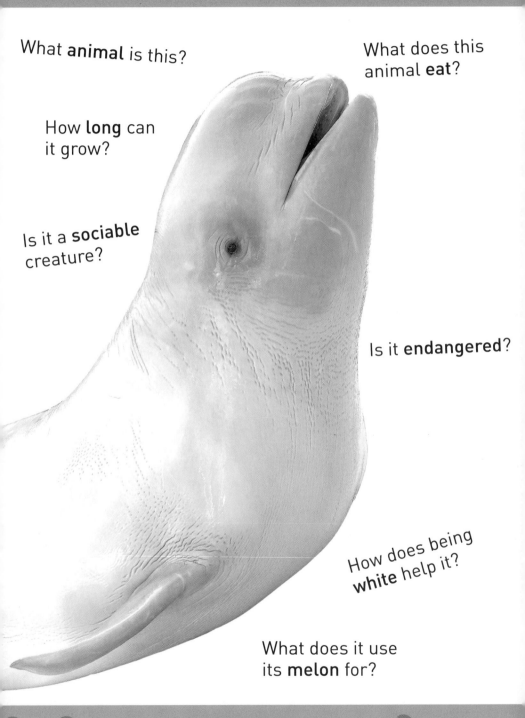

What **animal** is this?

What does this animal **eat**?

How **long** can it grow?

Is it a **sociable** creature?

Is it **endangered**?

How does being **white** help it?

What does it use its **melon** for?

# Beluga

Unique among whales for its white skin, the beluga lives in the icy waters of the Arctic where it feeds on fish, squid, and shellfish, such as crabs, and clams. Its skin color may be an adaptation to life among the floating sea ice, helping to conceal it from hungry enemies, such as killer whales and polar bears.

**Location** Arctic Ocean

**Habitat** ～～ ⚊

**Diet** Fish, mollusks, crustaceans

**Status** Least Concern

**Length** 10–14¾ ft (3–4.5 m)

The beluga's prominent forehead bulge contains an organ called a melon. It focuses echoes of the beluga's calls, helping it locate prey and other objects.

The thick layer of fat beneath a beluga's skin accounts for nearly half its body weight.

Belugas are very sociable animals. They live in small groups, or pods, typically made up of about ten adults and their young, but these may join to form huge herds of up to several thousand.

# Blood sucker

What **animal** is this?

What does this animal **eat**?

Where in the **world** does it live?

When does it **feed**?

Can it travel on the **ground**?

# Vampire bat

At night, the vampire bat flutters down near a target—usually a sleeping chicken, cow, or human—and quietly crawls closer, like a spider. The victim rarely feels the bat's sharp, pointed teeth bite and its tongue lapping the blood. The bite is not dangerous, but some bats transmit a deadly disease called rabies.

**Location** Mexico, South America

**Habitat**

**Diet** Blood of large mammals and birds

**Status** Least Concern

**Length** 2¼–3¾ in (7–10 cm)

The vampire bat is a strong flier, but it can also scuttle over the ground with speed and agility, propped up on its forearms and back legs.

Vampire bats look after other bats in their colony by feeding them when they're sick.

# Deadly hunter

What **animal** is this?

What is its natural **habitat**?

What is its **endangered** status?

Where does this animal **live**?

Where does it catch its **prey**?

Can it **swim**?

Where does it give **birth**?

# Polar bear

The record-breaking polar bear is the world's largest carnivore on land. It is an accomplished swimmer and moves with ease both on land and on slippery ice. Its fur is thicker than that of any other bear and acts as a useful camouflage in the snowy landscape.

**Location** Arctic, Canada

**Habitat** 🏔

**Diet** Seals, birds

**Status** Vulnerable

**Length** 6–9ft (1.8–2.8m)

Polar bears can run at 25 mph (40 kph) and swim at 6 mph (10 kph).

Polar bears are excellent swimmers and can travel for hundreds of miles in the water. Ice floes provide a base while the bear searches for seals in the Arctic Ocean.

In winter, female bears dig dens in the snow to give birth and protect their newborn cubs from the freezing temperatures. The dens are built on land, close to the coast for hunting.

# Bamboo eater

What **animal** is this?

What is this animal's **endangered** status?

What is its favorite **food**?

Can its **baby** take care of itself in the first few months?

What is its natural **habitat**?

How often does it give **birth**?

Where does it **live**?

# Giant panda

A familiar symbol of the world's endangered wildlife, the giant panda is under threat of extinction. It feeds almost exclusively on bamboo—a giant grass that grows abundantly in the forests of the panda's native central China. The giant panda is a bamboo-eating specialist that eats meat only very rarely.

**Location** Asia

**Habitat** 🌳 🌲 ⛰️

**Diet** Bamboo

**Status** Vulnerable

**Length** 4–6ft (1.2–1.8m)

Much of the bamboo the giant panda eats passes through its body without being digested, so it must eat a huge amount.

A thumb-like growth on the wrist bone allows the panda to grip bamboo stalks.

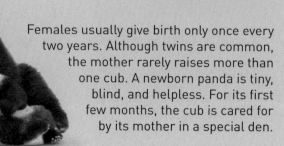

Females usually give birth only once every two years. Although twins are common, the mother rarely raises more than one cub. A newborn panda is tiny, blind, and helpless. For its first few months, the cub is cared for by its mother in a special den.

What **animal** is this?

Where in the **world** does this animal live?

The grizzly bear is a **subspecies**. True or false?

What is its **diet**?

How is its walk **different** from other carnivores?

How does it use its long **claws**?

# Brown bear

The brown bear enjoys the widest distribution of all bear species and varies widely in size depending on its food and habitat. Its distinctive features are its shoulder hump of muscle, and long claws that help it dig for roots and bulbs. In North America, a subspecies of the brown bear is known as the grizzly bear.

**Location** US, Europe, Asia

**Habitat**

**Diet** Fruit, plants, small mammals, fish

**Status** Least Concern

**Length** 5–9 ft (1.5–2.8 m)

A bear walks on the sole of its feet, not the toes like most carnivores.

The brown bear can stand upright on its hind paws in order to identify a threat or a food source.

In coastal Alaska, grizzly bears catch salmon that swim upriver from the sea. The bears gather in large numbers at some sites, with the biggest males claiming the best fishing spots.

# Distinctive stripes

What **animal** is this?

Where does it **live**?

Does it live in **herds**?

What might its **stripes** be for?

What does it **eat**?

How many **toes** does it have?

**Mammals**
*Equus quagga*

# Plains zebra

Beneath its stripes, the plains zebra has all the familiar features of horses—a long muzzle so it can graze while watching for danger, big chewing teeth, long legs, and hooves. The reason for its stripes is unknown, but they may help the herd to blend in as one, keep the animal cool, or ward off insect bites.

**Location** Africa

**Habitat** 🌿

**Diet** Grass, leaves, buds

**Status** Near Threatened

**Length** 7¼–8¼ ft (2.2–2.5 m)

The plains zebra is the only zebra with stripes under its belly. It is the most common and widespread type of zebra. Herds of several hundred animals are a familiar sight.

Even lions and cheetahs can be injured or killed by large male zebras in a battle.

The ancestors of zebras had three or more toes. But after millions of years of evolution, only one toe on each foot remains, capped by a strong hoof. The result is a tough, shock-absorbing foot ideal for running.

# Wild one

What **animal** is this?

What is its natural **habitat**?

Where was it **discovered**?

Is this animal **endangered**?

Where in the **world** does this animal live?

Why is **grooming** important to it?

**Mammals**
*Equus przewalskii*

# Przewalski's horse

Przewalski's horse is the only surviving truly wild horse that is closely related to domestic horses. It was identified in 1881 in western Mongolia by Russian explorer Colonel Nicolai Przewalski, but was almost wiped out in the 20th century. Having been reintroduced to their native range, Przewalski's horses appear to be slowly increasing in numbers.

**Location** Central Asia

**Habitat**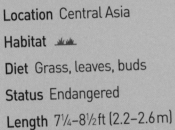

**Diet** Grass, leaves, buds

**Status** Endangered

**Length** 7¼–8½ ft (2.2–2.6 m)

Social grooming is important for Przewalski's horse, as it reinforces herd bonds. Usually two horses stand nose to tail so they can look out for danger in both directions, and each nibbles the other's shoulder.

These horses have sharp frontal teeth shaped like chisels for slicing up grass.

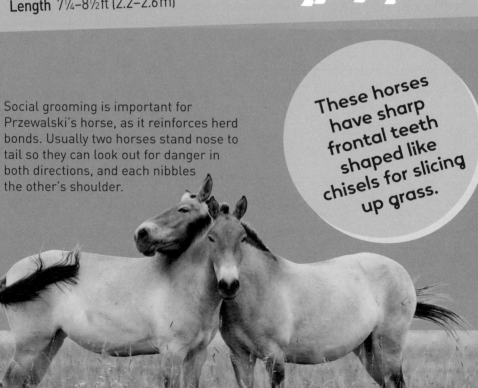

What **animal** is this?

Where does it **live**?

What other **name** is it called?

Can it **see** well?

When does it usually **feed**?

How does it **protect** itself against the sun?

Is this animal **endangered**?

# Black rhino

The black rhino feeds mainly on bushes and low trees, and is normally found in wooded savanna—a habitat with a mixture of grass and trees. Its sight is poor but it has excellent hearing and smell. The black rhino feeds mostly at night, and spends its days dozing in shade or wallowing in mud.

**Location** Africa

**Habitat**

**Diet** Grass, twigs, leaves

**Status** Critically Endangered

**Length** 9½–10ft (2.9–3.1m)

Rhinos cover themselves in layers of mud as protection against the sun.

The black rhino, also known as the hook-lipped rhinoceros, has a pointed upper lip. This curls around twigs to draw them into the mouth, where they are bitten off by the teeth.

The female gives birth after 15–16 months' gestation. The newborn weighs around 88 lb (40 kg), begins to take solid food after a few weeks, and is weaned at around two years.

# Armor plated

What **animal** is this?

Is it **endangered**?

What is this animal's natural **habitat**?

How **long** does it grow?

How does it **protect** itself?

How does it **chew** its food?

What are its **scales** made from?

When is it most **active**?

**Mammals**
*Manis temminckii*

# Ground pangolin

The ground pangolin is covered in scales, which act as armor and camouflage. Because it lacks teeth, prey is collected with the tongue, and powerful muscles in the stomach "chew" the food. The pangolin rips open termite mounds and ant nests, both in trees and on the ground, with its large claws.

**Location** Africa

**Habitat**

**Diet** Ants, termites

**Status** Vulnerable

**Length** 18–21½ in (45–55 cm)

When ground pangolins are threatened, they can curl up into a ball, with the sharp edges of their large scales providing additional defense.

A pangolin's scales are modified hairs, made of keratin and fused together.

The ground pangolin is very secretive. It is nocturnal and walks on four feet, or two if it's foraging for food.

# Super snout

What **animal** is this?

Where does it **live**?

When is this animal **active**?

What does it **eat**?

What is its **tongue** coated with?

How does it **protect** its front claws?

How big can its home **range** be?

# Giant anteater

The giant anteater has a long, tubular snout that widens to a small face with small ears and eyes. With its massive front legs and smaller rear legs, the giant anteater walks with an ambling gait, protecting its large front claws by walking on its knuckles. It is threatened by hunting and habitat destruction.

**Location** Central America, South America

**Habitat**

**Diet** Ants, termites

**Status** Vulnerable

**Length** 3¼–6½ ft (1–2 m)

An anteater's sharp front claws can be lethal against even jaguars.

The giant anteater rips open ant nests and termite mounds with its claws, and uses its tongue, which can extend more than 2 ft (60 cm), to take its prey. The tongue is coated with spines and sticky saliva to help it catch prey.

Active day and night, the giant anteater wanders its home range, which may cover up to 10 square miles (25 square km), depending on the availability of food.

# Slow mover

What **animal** is this?

What is its natural **habitat**?

Where in the **world** does this animal live?

How often does it **move** from the trees to the ground?

What is its **diet**?

Can it **swim**?

Why does it sometimes turn a **green** color?

**Mammals**
*Choloepus didactylus*

# Southern two-toed sloth

The southern two-toed sloth is a herbivore. It has no incisors or canines, only cylindrical, rootless teeth that are used to grind up food. The two-toed sloth can swim well, even crossing rivers. It is solitary, moves extremely slowly, and descends to the ground only to defecate (about once a week).

**Location** South America

**Habitat**

**Diet** Leaves, fruit

**Status** Least Concern

**Length** 18–34 in (46–86 cm)

A sloth can take a month to completely digest a meal.

The coarse, bushy fur of the southern two-toed sloth is grayish-brown, and paler on the face. It may be tinged green by algae growing on the hairs.

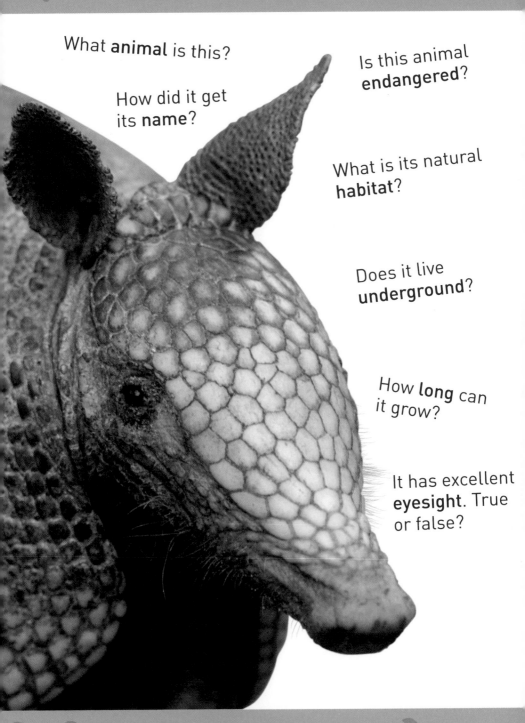

# Little banded one

What **animal** is this?

How did it get its **name**?

Is this animal **endangered**?

What is its natural **habitat**?

Does it live **underground**?

How **long** can it grow?

It has excellent **eyesight**. True or false?

# Nine-banded armadillo

The name armadillo comes from the Spanish for "little banded one" and refers to the protective bony plates coated in horny skin that cover the animals' back. This armor and leathery skin account for one-sixth of the nine-banded armadillo's total weight. Like most armadillos, it digs an extensive burrow system.

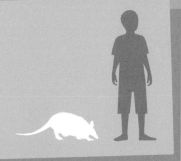

**Location** US, South America, Caribbean

**Habitat** 

**Diet** Ants, birds, fruit

**Status** Least Concern

**Length** 14–22½ in (35–57 cm)

The nine-banded armadillo is solitary. However, it may share a burrow with others of its kind.

The armadillo's poor eyesight means that it relies on its nose when hunting.

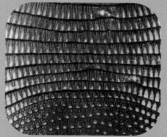

The nine-banded armadillo is named for the nine bands of bony plates across its back.

# Big-eyed jumper

What **animal** is this?

Where does this animal **live**?

Does it live in big **groups**?

What does it **eat**?

When does it **hunt**?

How far can it **jump**?

What does it use to **moisten** its hands and feet?

**Mammals**
*Galago moholi*

# Moholi bush baby

The moholi bush baby is also called the lesser bush baby. It snatches insects from midair by hand or scrapes gum from trees with its comblike lower front teeth. Its grasping hands and feet are moistened regularly with urine to maintain grip. It lives in small family groups, which sleep huddled together by day.

**Location** Africa

**Habitat**

**Diet** Tree gum, insects

**Status** Least Concern

**Length** 4¾–6½ in (12–17 cm)

Their round heads have very large eyes, which help them see at night while hunting for insects.

A bush baby's large ears can move independently of each other, which is useful for hunting.

The moholi bush baby can make enormous jumps of 16 ft (5 m) using its powerful legs.

122

# Graceful goliath

What **animal** is this?

What is this animal's natural **habitat**?

How **wide** can it open its mouth?

What is its **diet**?

Why are its **nostrils** high on its head?

Does it have big **teeth**?

# Common hippopotamus

Despite its massive bulk, the hippopotamus walks underwater with grace and trots surprisingly fast on land on its short legs. Its skin has a thin outer layer, which dries out easily and is sensitive to the bites of pests such as flies. Hippopotamuses have been known to attack humans if they feel threatened.

**Location** Africa

**Habitat** 🌿🌱〰️〰️

**Diet** Grass

**Status** Vulnerable

**Length** 9½–16 ft (2.9–5.1 m)

The hippopotamus's nostrils, eyes, and ears are all on top of its head, so it can be almost submerged yet breathe easily.

The hippo's lower teeth grind against the upper ones, sharpening them.

Hippopotamuses have a long body with short legs. The enormous head features jaws that allow a huge gape (up to 150 degrees).

What **animal** is this?

Is it **endangered**?

Where does it build **nests**?

Is its bill very **heavy**?

How does it impress a potential **mate**?

What does it **eat**?

Where in the **world** does it live?

**Birds**
*Ramphastos toco*

# Toco toucan

The toco toucan is the largest of all toucans. The function of its distinctive bill is not clear, although its length is useful for plucking fruit, and its bright color may be used to impress other toucans. It is also used in courtship rituals, where a toucan will toss fruit to a potential mate to start a game of catch.

**Location** South America

**Habitat**

**Diet** Fruit, eggs, small animals

**Status** Least Concern

**Length** 21–23½ in (53–60 cm)

The large bill helps the toco toucan reach food. Once collected, food is moved from the tip of the bill to the throat with a toss of the head.

The toco toucan builds nests inside holes in trees, earth banks, or termite mounds.

The inside of a toucan's bill is a honeycomb-like structure, making it much lighter.

# Loud drummer

What **animal** is this?

What is this animal's natural **habitat**?

Is there a difference in the **coloring** of the male and female?

What does it use its **bill** for?

What does its **call** sound like?

What does it **eat**?

Why are its strong **feet** important?

# Great spotted woodpecker

Like other woodpeckers, great spotted woodpeckers forage their way up tree trunks, with their tail braced for support. They lift the bark with their bill and probe underneath with a long, sticky tongue. They also hack into wood to dig out insect grubs and occasionally steal young birds from their nests.

**Location** Africa, Asia, Europe

**Habitat** 🌳 🌲 🏠

**Diet** Ants, birds, fruit

**Status** Least Concern

**Length** 8–9½ in (20–24 cm)

The female resembles the male but lacks a red patch on the back of the head.

A great spotted woodpecker makes a regular metallic "chik" call.

The woodpecker's strong feet keep it anchored while it hammers into trees. Early in the breeding season, its loud drumming sound can be heard.

# Iridescent tail

What **animal** is this?

Is it **endangered**?

What is the **female** called?

Where in the **world** does it live?

How many **feathers** does the male have in its tail?

How does the male **court** the female?

**Birds**
*Pavo cristatus*

# Indian peacock

The Indian peacock (also known as the Indian peafowl) is a well-known ornamental bird. The male has a metallic blue body and about 150 huge feathers in its tail. When the male is courting, these feathers are spread out like a fan, revealing a colorful collection of iridescent eyespots in copper and green tones.

**Location** Asia

**Habitat**

**Diet** Seeds, insects, small reptiles

**Status** Least Concern

**Length** 6–7½ ft (1.8–2.3 m)

During the breeding season, the male fans its train to impress females. After mating, the male leaves the female to nest and incubate the eggs on her own.

A peacock scratches the soil with its strong feet for insects and seeds.

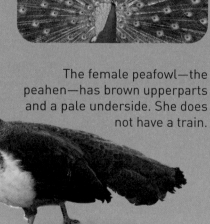

The female peafowl—the peahen—has brown upperparts and a pale underside. She does not have a train.

# Soaring scavenger

What **animal** is this?

What does this animal **eat**?

Does it have good **vision**?

What is its natural **habitat**?

Is it **endangered**?

Where does this animal **nest**?

How long does its **young** stay in the nest?

How does it get its **name**?

**Birds**

*Gyps africanus*

# White-backed vulture

This widespread African scavenger has a feather-free face that allows it to reach deep into carcasses without getting dirty. The white-backed vulture makes hissing and cackling sounds as it jostles with rivals for a chance to eat. It gets its name from a collar of white feathers at the top of its back.

**Location** Africa

**Habitat** 🌾 ⛰️ 🌵 🌳

**Diet** Carrion

**Status** Critically Endangered

**Length** 37 in (94 cm)

White-backed vultures have excellent vision and can spot a carcass from miles away, often by spying on the movement of other vultures.

A vulture will timidly wait for other animals to open up a fresh carcass.

They nest in large trees, making a platform of sticks and lining it with grass and leaves. Their young stay in the nest for 17 weeks.

What **animal** is this?

Where does it make its **nest**?

Does it live in a small **flock**?

How does it **find** its food?

Where in the **world** does it live?

What is its natural **habitat**?

Where does it **roost** at night?

**Birds**
*Eudocimus ruber*

# Scarlet ibis

The vividly colored scarlet ibis gathers in large flocks—sometimes numbering tens of thousands of birds. In the breeding season, it is found in the coastal wetlands of Latin America, such as swamps, lagoons, mangroves, and tidal rivers. Birds of a colony pair for breeding, building their nests in trees close to water.

**Location** Central America, South America

**Habitat**

**Diet** Crabs, shellfish, aquatic insects

**Status** Least Concern

**Length** 22–27 in (56–68 cm)

The scarlet ibis feeds on the ground during the day, but at dusk it flies into trees to roost, safely out of reach of most predators.

Scarlet ibises prefer to nest on islands, where they are safer from predators.

The scarlet ibis finds its food primarily by touch instead of by sight, probing into soft mud with its long, curved bill, usually while walking.

# Dazzling feathers

What **animal** is this?

What protects its **eyes** underwater?

What does this animal **eat**?

How does it **catch** its prey?

How does it get rid of **undigested** food?

What is its **endangered** status?

Where does it **live**?

**Birds**
*Alcedo atthis*

# Common kingfisher

The common kingfisher is the only kingfisher found in most of Europe. It is a small, swift, and active bird with a cinnamon-colored underside; greenish-blue crown, back, and wings; and dazzling, cobalt-blue rump and tail. The common kingfisher's sharp bill is well-adapted for striking and grasping fish.

**Location** Africa, Asia, Europe

**Habitat** 🍄🌾〰️🪵🏠〰️

**Diet** Small fish

**Status** Least Concern

**Length** 6½ in (16 cm)

Having captured its prey by a dramatic dive, the common kingfisher then takes it back to its perch, on which it strikes the fish repeatedly before swallowing it headfirst. Any undigested remains are usually regurgitated as pellets.

A kingfisher has a transparent third eyelid, which protects its eyes underwater.

# Pure white plumage

What **animal** is this?

What is its natural **habitat**?

At what age do its **babies** become independent?

What is its **diet**?

How does it **reach** food in underwater mud?

What **color** are its babies?

# Mute swan

The mute swan is one of the world's heaviest flying birds. It runs or paddles across water to take off, but once airborne, the mute swan is a powerful flier, making a pulsating sound with its wings. When young, it is gray, but the adult has pure white plumage, a reddish bill, and black legs and feet.

**Location** US, Europe, Africa, Asia, Australia

**Habitat**

**Diet** Small animals, aquatic plants

**Status** Least Concern

**Length** 5ft (1.5m)

Both parents care for the young mute swans until they become independent at about five months. It takes three to four years for them to become fully mature.

Mute swans feed mainly when in water, often upending to reach plants and small animals in underwater mud.

Some mute swan wingspans stretch to more than 6½ ft (2m).

What **animal** is this?

Where in the **world** does it live?

What does it **eat**?

Is it **endangered**?

What does its **call** sound like?

Do the male and female look **different**?

How long does a **baby** stay with its parents?

**Birds**
*Dacelo novaeguineae*

# Laughing kookaburra

Famous for its humanlike laughing call, this stocky bird is one of Australia's best-known birds. It is a relative of the kingfisher, and hunts by sitting perched on a branch while keeping a watchful eye on the ground for prey. The laughing kookaburra eats anything it can swoop on and overpower, such as insects.

**Location** Australia, New Zealand

**Habitat**

**Diet** Insects, snakes, small birds

**Status** Least Concern

**Length** 16½ in (42 cm)

The laughing kookaburra's noisy call is often heard at dawn and dusk—several others may then join in!

Male and female laughing kookaburras are almost identical.

Young birds take more than a month to grow their plumage. They stay with their parents for a year or more.

What **animal** is this?

What is this animal's natural **habitat**?

What is its **diet**?

Do both parents help **raise** the young?

How far does it **migrate**?

How does the male **court** the female?

# Ruby-throated hummingbird

The ruby-throated hummingbird lives in forests, frequents backyard hummingbird feeders, and drinks the nectar of wildflowers. Males arrive at breeding grounds first and court females with high-speed display flights. They mate with several partners in a season and take no part in raising the young.

**Location** North America, Central America

**Habitat**

**Diet** Insects, nectar

**Status** Least Concern

**Length** 3½ in (9 cm)

Females raise the young on their own. Incubation lasts about 16 days, and the young fatten up rapidly. This is essential preparation for their migration across the Gulf of Mexico—a nonstop flight of more than 500 miles (800 km).

A hummingbird's wings can beat up to 200 times a second, making a humming noise in the process.

# Flightless sprinter

What **animal** is this?

Where in the **world** does this animal live?

How **fast** can it run?

Why does it **swallow** stones?

Is it **endangered**?

How is it a **record** breaker?

What **color** is the female?

# Common ostrich

The ostrich lives in the deserts and grasslands of Africa and is the world's tallest and heaviest bird. It escapes enemies by running on its unique, two-toed feet and can sprint at up to 45 mph (70 kph). Although flightless, it has large wings, which it spreads during courtship displays and to keep cool.

**Location** Africa

**Habitat**

**Diet** Plants, grass

**Status** Least Concern

**Length** 7–9¼ft (2.1–2.8m)

Ostriches swallow stones as big as golf balls to help grind their food.

Male ostriches compete for territory and social status with aggressive displays and occasionally by fighting. The winner gains territory and several females.

The female ostrich is grayish-brown, without any white in its plumage.

# Long-billed burrower

What **animal** is this?

Is it **endangered**?

What does it **eat**?

What **difference** is there between the male and female?

Where in the **world** does this animal live?

When does it look for **food**?

How does it find its **prey**?

**Birds**
*Apteryx mantelli*

# North Island brown kiwi

North Island brown kiwis share their origins with other flightless birds and are most closely related to emus and cassowaries. Kiwis need high humidity; well-drained soil for digging nesting burrows and daytime dens; and moist leaf litter in which to find food such as insects, worms, and grubs at night.

**Location** New Zealand

**Habitat**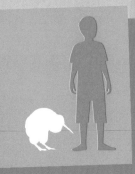

**Diet** Insects, worms, millipedes

**Status** Vulnerable

**Length** 20–26 in (50–65 cm)

Females are bigger than males and produce eggs four times as large as might be expected for the bird's size.

Only 5 percent of kiwis survive to reach adulthood.

North Island brown kiwis detect prey by sound, smell, and touch, leaving a trail of holes where they have probed with their bill.

# Tundra dweller

What **animal** is this?

What is its natural **habitat**?

Where does this animal **live**?

Where does the female make a **nest**?

How does it find its **prey** in the snow?

Is the male or female **larger**?

**Birds**
*Bubo scandiacus*

# Snowy owl

The snowy owl is beautifully insulated and superbly camouflaged. Its thick plumage covers its entire body, including its nostrils and toes, and its white color makes it very difficult to spot against a background of rocks and snow. The young male and female snowy owls are similar, but males become whiter as they age.

**Location** Arctic

**Habitat** 🌱 🏞️ ⛰️

**Diet** Small mammals

**Status** Least Concern

**Length** 22–28 in (55–70 cm)

Female snowy owls nest on the tundra, laying their eggs in a hollow on the ground. They feed their young with food brought by the male.

A snowy owl hunts by listening for its preys' movements under the snow.

Larger than the male, the female snowy owl has black flecks on its feathers and a speckled crown, which provide camouflage when nesting.

# Fish snatcher

What **animal** is this?

Where in the **world** does this animal live?

What is its main **diet**?

Is it a **solitary** creature?

How big is its **nest**?

How does it catch its **prey**?

# Bald eagle

One of the world's largest birds of prey, the bald eagle is heavily built, with a conspicuous white head and strong legs with grasping talons. Bald eagles mainly feed on fish. Every year they gather in large numbers along salmon rivers, waiting to feast on fish that have come upstream to spawn.

Location US

Habitat

Diet Fish, birds, carrion

Status Least Concern

Length 25–38 in (71–96 cm)

The bald eagle is easily spotted by its pure white head, and its broad wings. It uses its sharp claws to snatch fish from the water's surface.

Bald eagle nests can be up to 13 ft (4 m) tall.

Bald eagles mate for life. They build an extremely large stick nest, adding to it year after year until it weighs several tons.

What **animal** is this?

What is its natural **habitat**?

Is it **endangered**?

Where does it **live**?

How does it use its **neck** fan?

What does it do when it is **excited** or alarmed?

Is it a **solitary** creature?

**Birds**
*Deroptyus accipitrinus*

# Red-fan parrot

Parrots are celebrated for their intelligence and ability to mimic human speech. They are colorful birds with powerful, hooked bills for cracking seeds and nuts. While perching, red-fan parrots resemble birds of prey, with their hawklike eyes. They are usually seen in pairs or small groups.

**Location** South America

**Habitat**

**Diet** Seeds, nuts

**Status** Least Concern

**Length** 14 in (35 cm)

Red-fan parrots have distinctive dark red feathers, which extend from the nape to the hind neck. When excited or alarmed, they raise their neck feathers to form a spectacular ruff or fan.

The ruff or fan makes the parrot look larger and helps scare off predators.

# Flock-forming screecher

What **animal** is this?

Where does this animal **live**?

What does it **eat**?

When does it open its **crest** like a fan?

How does it use its **bill**?

Where does it **nest**?

# Sulfur-crested cockatoo

A medium-size bird with a harsh, screeching call, the sulfur-crested cockatoo is a common sight across much of its range. It has white plumage and a distinctive yellow crest. The crest opens like a fan when the bird is alarmed or carrying out a display. These flock-forming parrots roost and breed in trees.

**Location** New Guinea, Australia

**Habitat**

**Diet** Seeds

**Status** Least Concern

**Length** 20in (50cm)

Their bills are multipurpose tools, used to collect seeds, dig up roots, climb, and tear off strips of wood.

A cockatoo can use one foot to hold food and the other to break pieces off.

Sulfur-crested cockatoos are cavity nesters. They lay their eggs in hollows lined with debris, high in eucalyptus trees. The parents share the task of incubation, and both bring food to the chicks.

# Multicolored bill

What **animal** is this?

What is its natural **habitat**?

Where does it **live**?

How **deep** can it dive?

Can it **fly**?

How does it hold lots of **fish** at the same time?

Is it **endangered**?

# Atlantic puffin

The puffin is the most colorful seabird in the North Atlantic, with a multicolored bill and bright orange legs and feet. It sometimes dives 200 ft (60 m) underwater to find the shoaling fish that are its main food. To nest, the puffin digs a burrow in the ground and lines it with feathers and plant matter.

**Location** North Atlantic, Arctic Ocean

**Habitat**

**Diet** Fish

**Status** Vulnerable

**Length** 11–12 in (28–30 cm)

Atlantic puffins are highly social. On land they stand in groups, and when feeding in the sea they float together in large flocks (rafts).

A puffin's short wings act as flippers underwater but are long enough for flight.

The Atlantic puffin's upper bill and tongue are ridged with spikes that enable it to hold lots of slippery fish at the same time.

What **animal** is this?

What is this animal's natural **habitat**?

What is its **diet**?

Where does it **lay** its eggs?

Is it **endangered**?

How does a **chick** get the food it needs?

**Birds**
*Cuculus canorus*

# Common cuckoo

The common cuckoo is a brood parasite—a bird that tricks other bird species into raising its young. The process begins after mating, when the female cuckoo searches for the nests of smaller birds. Waiting until the owners are absent, it removes an egg and replaces it with one of its own.

**Location** Africa, Asia, Europe

**Habitat** 🌳🌳 🌲🌲🌲

**Diet** Invertebrates

**Status** Least Concern

**Length** 13 in (33 cm)

After hatching, a cuckoo chick is large and strong enough to eject any other eggs or chicks in the nest. It soon outgrows its adult carers, which never realize they are feeding an impostor.

A common cuckoo has the "cooc-coo" call that gives cuckoos their name.

# Elegant wader

What **animal** is this?

Where does it **live**?

What does it **eat**?

Why does it stand on **one** leg?

How far can it **fly** to find food?

How does it **court** its mate?

How many can live in a **group**?

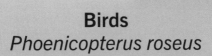

**Birds**
*Phoenicopterus roseus*

# Greater flamingo

The greater flamingo is found in a wide variety of freshwater and saltwater habitats, particularly salt lakes, estuaries, and lagoons. Its large size enables it to wade out into relatively deep water to reach food. In flocks, they may fly great distances—up to 300 miles (500 km)—to find new feeding sites.

**Location** Latin America, Europe, Asia, Africa

**Habitat**

**Diet** Small animals, algae

**Status** Least Concern

**Length** 5 ft (1.5 m)

Females lay a single egg in a nest that looks like a miniature mud volcano.

The greater flamingo often stands on one leg for long periods, even when asleep. This posture cuts heat loss through the legs and feet.

Greater flamingos breed in colonies of up to 200,000 monogamous pairs. Courtship involves complex, synchronized dances.

# Swift diver

What **animal** is this?

How does it **catch** its prey?

Why is this animal a **record** breaker?

Is it **endangered**?

Where does it **nest**?

How many **chicks** does it raise a year?

**Birds**
*Falco peregrinus*

# Peregrine falcon

The world's fastest bird, the peregrine falcon is a relentless predator that dive-bombs other birds in a spectacular plunge known as a stoop. With its wings folded by its sides, the peregrine drops vertically, slashing prey in midair with talons, and catching the victim as it tumbles to the ground.

**Location** Worldwide (except Antarctica)

**Habitat**

**Diet** A variety of birds

**Status** Least Concern

**Length** 13½–20 in (34–50 cm)

Peregrine falcons live in many different habitats, from rocky coasts to city centers. They nest on rocky ledges and raise two to four chicks a year.

A peregrine falcon is one of the fastest moving animals on Earth.

The peregrine falcon chases prey, such as doves, to exhaustion. After catching its kill, the falcon flies to a perch to dismember it.

# Trailing plumage

What **animal** is this?

Is it a type of **heron**?

It lives in **Antarctica**. True or false?

When does it develop long back **plumes**?

Is it a **social** creature?

How do the **chicks** behave in the nest?

What does it **eat**?

**Birds**
*Ardea alba*

# Great egret

The great egret is the most widespread of all herons. Its plumage is entirely white, and its legs and feet are black. In the breeding season, long plumes develop on the back, trailing over the relatively short tail. Unlike other egrets, the great egret prefers to forage alone and defends its territory from other wading birds.

**Location** Worldwide (except Antarctica)

**Habitat**

**Diet** Fish, crustaceans

**Status** Least Concern

**Length** 34–39 in (85–100 cm)

The great egret points its bill to the sky and shows off its "aigrettes" (delicate feathers), which are present only when it's breeding.

The great egret's young in the nest are extremely aggressive, often resulting in the death of weaker chicks.

The great egret waits patiently for fish and frogs, then suddenly spears them with its beak.

# Superbly streamlined

What **animal** is this?

What is its natural **habitat**?

Where in the **world** does this animal live?

What **noise** does it make when flying?

Where does it **nest**?

How many **eggs** does the female lay?

How far does it **migrate** every year?

**Birds**
*Hirundo rustica*

# Barn swallow

Barn swallows undertake some of the longest journeys of any migrating songbird. Every year they migrate thousands of miles between their feeding grounds in the tropics and breeding sites throughout the northern hemisphere. They are superbly streamlined, with a wide gape for catching insects in flight.

**Location** US, Africa, Europe

**Habitat**

**Diet** Insects

**Status** Least Concern

**Length** 7in (18cm)

These migrant songbirds often return to where they bred the previous year. They utter a chuckling twitter when flying.

A male swallow has longer tail feathers (tail streamers) than the female.

Barn swallows nest in barns and other open-sided rafters or beams. Females lay four to six eggs, which are incubated for up to 16 days.

# Sleek hunter

What **animal** is this?

What is its **diet**?

Is it **endangered**?

Where does it **live**?

Does the male or female **incubate** the egg?

How long can it stay **underwater**?

Where does it **breed**?

# Emperor penguin

The emperor penguin is a sleek hunter that dives under the Antarctic ice to catch fish and squid. Emperors breed on sea ice. The female lays a single egg, then returns to open waters to feed. The male incubates the egg, waiting patiently for his mate to return before making the long journey across the ice to feed.

**Location** Antarctica

**Habitat** 〰️🏔️🌊

**Diet** Fish, squid, krill

**Status** Near Threatened

**Length** 3½ft (1.1m)

An emperor penguin can stay underwater for up to 20 minutes.

All winter, the male guards the egg, which sits on his feet, covered with a fold of skin to prevent the egg from freezing. While the male incubates the egg, he does not eat, losing up to half his body weight over two months.

What **animal** is this?

How **long** does it grow?

How **deep** can it dive?

What is this animal's natural **habitat**?

How long can it stay **underwater**?

Why does it look **whitewashed**?

**Reptiles**
*Amblyrhynchus cristatus*

# Marine iguana

The marine iguana, with its large, scaly head and back, is the only lizard that forages for food in the sea. It dives for algae in the cold sea, and its body is specially adapted to cope both with cold and with excess salt. Large adults may dive down to 39 ft (12 m) and can stay underwater for more than an hour.

**Location** Galapagos Islands

**Habitat** 🏝️ 〰️

**Diet** Red and green algae

**Status** Vulnerable

**Length** 20–39 in (50–100 cm)

During the breeding season, males fight aggressively for the opportunity to mate.

Most marine iguanas have a "whitewashed" look, which comes from salt expelled by their nasal glands.

A blunt snout allows a marine iguana to graze on underwater seaweed.

What **animal** is this?

Where does it **live**?

What does it **eat**?

What does it do when it is **threatened**?

Where does it **forage**?

Can it **climb**?

**Reptiles**
*Chlamydosaurus kingii*

# Frilled lizard

The frilled lizard is one of Australia's most spectacular creatures. Its name derives from the large, leathery frill around its neck, which is normally folded back over its shoulders. However, if the lizard is threatened, it opens the frill like an umbrella, and rocks its body and hisses through its gaping mouth.

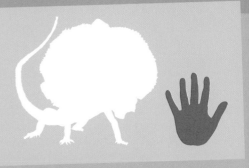

**Location** New Guinea, Australia

**Habitat**

**Diet** Insects, spiders

**Status** Least Concern

**Length** 23½–28in (60–70cm)

Frilled lizards forage mainly on the ground. They are good climbers, and after carrying out their defensive display they usually scuttle up a tree trunk to the highest branch.

A frilled lizard runs on two legs when fleeing from a predator.

# Heavy wrestler

What **animal** is this?

Is it **endangered**?

How **long** does it grow?

Where in the **world** does this animal live?

What is its average **weight**?

Why is its **saliva** dangerous?

How many **eggs** does the female lay?

How does the male **compete** for a mate?

**Reptiles**
*Varanus komodoensis*

# Komodo dragon

With an average weight of about 155 lb (70 kg), and sometimes double this in captivity, the Komodo dragon is the world's heaviest lizard. It has a forked tongue, which it flicks out as it searches for food. Young Komodo dragons are marked with gray or cream bands, but lose these markings as they mature.

**Location** Indonesia

**Habitat** 🌿

**Diet** Live animals, carrion

**Status** Endangered

**Length** 6½–9¾ ft (2–3 m)

A Komodo dragon's drooling saliva is laced with venom.

During the breeding season, males compete for the chance to mate, wrestling in an upright position propped against their tails. After mating, females dig nests in sandy ground, laying clutches of up to 25 eggs.

# Dewlap display

What **animal** is this?

What is this animal's natural **habitat**?

What is its **diet**?

What does it use the **dewlap** for?

Can it **swim**?

How much does it usually **weigh**?

**Reptiles**
*Iguana iguana*

# Green iguana

The green iguana is one of the largest lizards in the Americas. It is generally gray or green, although some vary in shades of orange. It has stout legs, a long tail, and a crest of toothlike scales down its back. Adults also have a fleshy dewlap beneath the throat, which is larger in males.

**Location** Central America, South America

**Habitat** 🌳

**Diet** Fruit, flowers, leaves, insects

**Status** Least Concern

**Length** 3¼–6½ft (1–2m)

The male is easily identified by the large dewlap beneath his throat, used for mating displays. Adult males are highly territorial.

Iguanas can swim, using their tail to propel them through the water.

The average green iguana weighs up to 11 lb (5 kg). Despite their predatory appearance, adults are almost entirely herbivorous, often feeding in trees.

# Toxic bite

What **animal** is this?

Where does
it **live**?

Is it **endangered**?

How does it **hunt**?

Does it **move** quickly?

Where does
it **store** fat?

How **long** does it grow?

Can it **burrow**?

**Reptiles**
*Heloderma suspectum*

# Gila monster

The Gila monster is one of only two dangerously venomous lizards in the world. Its bulky body is marked with pink or yellow, contrasting with bands of black warning potential attackers that it has a toxic bite. Gila monsters live in semi-desert areas with rocky outcrops, in places where they can access water.

**Location** US, Mexico

**Habitat**

**Diet** Small mammals, eggs

**Status** Near Threatened

**Length** 14–20 in (35–50 cm)

This lizard has powerful limbs for burrowing and walks with a slow, lumbering gait. Its coloration acts as camouflage, and as a warning to predators.

The Gila monster feeds on small mammals and the eggs of birds and reptiles. It hunts by smell and also "tastes" its surroundings with its tongue.

After a large meal, this lizard stores fat in its tail.

# Crested camouflage

What **animal** is this?

What is its natural **habitat**?

Where in the **world** does this animal live?

How can you tell a male and female **apart**?

What does it **eat**?

How does it avoid **predators**?

**Reptiles**
*Trioceros jacksonii*

# Jackson's chameleon

With their three forward-pointing horns, males of this species are among the most distinctive of all chameleons. Their normal color is green, but those that live in East Africa's mountain forests are usually brighter and larger. The Jackson's chameleon relies on its camouflage to avoid being attacked.

**Location** Africa, Hawaii

**Habitat**

**Diet** Worms, insects

**Status** Least Concern

**Length** 8–12 in (20–30 cm)

A chameleon's tongue strikes prey within one tenth of a second.

Male and female Jackson's chameleons are easily told apart. The female is usually stockier than the male, and the horns are tiny or absent.

# Specialized hunter

What **animal** is this?

How **long** can it grow?

Where does it **live**?

Is it **endangered**?

Can it **kill** other snakes?

How many **eggs** does the female lay?

What does it do when it is **threatened**?

**Reptiles**
*Ophiophagus hannah*

# King cobra

The king cobra is the longest venomous snake and a specialized hunter of other snakes. It sometimes reaches a length of more than 16 ft (5 m), which allows it to overpower and kill other snakes of a considerable size. When threatened, it raises the front of its body and displays its narrow hood.

**Location** Asia

**Habitat**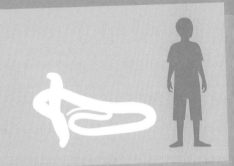

**Diet** Snakes, mice, rats

**Status** Vulnerable

**Length** 9¾–16 ft (3–5 m)

A king cobra's bite contains enough venom to kill an Asian elephant.

Females lay 21–40 eggs, which are guarded by both parents until they hatch.

Slender and smooth-scaled, the king cobra is a good swimmer and is often found near water. Adults are plain brown, while the young are darker and have pale markings on their front.

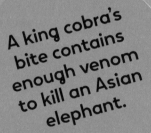

# Powerful squeeze

What **animal** is this?

What is this animal's natural **habitat**?

What is its **diet**?

How does it **detect** prey?

How does it **kill** its prey?

Where does it **live**?

What type of **markings** does it have?

**Reptiles**
*Boa constrictor*

# Common boa

A large snake, with a narrow head and a pointed snout, the common boa varies in color but has dark saddle markings along the back, sometimes becoming dark red toward the tail. It is very adaptable and uses a huge range of habitats—from tropical forest to dry savanna. It may also be found in urban areas.

**Location** Central America, South America

**Habitat** 

**Diet** Mammals, birds

**Status** Least Concern

**Length** 3½–13 ft (1–4 m)

Boas detect prey using scent rather than heat.

The common boa will sit and wait, watching its prey carefully. Timing its strike to perfection, it lunges forward and seizes its victim in its jaws before wrapping itself around it. The snake suffocates its prey by tightly squeezing it—a process that can be so quick that small animals may be killed in seconds.

# Animal ambusher

What **animal** is this?

Is it **endangered**?

How much can it **weigh**?

How does it **kill** its prey?

What is the **largest** size of animal it can kill?

How long can it go **between** meals?

When does it usually **hunt**?

# Green anaconda

With a maximum weight of up to 550 lb (250 kg), the green anaconda is the world's heaviest snake. It spends most of its life partially submerged in shallow water. Green anacondas hunt mainly after dark. They lie in wait for mammals such as capybaras and deer, and can even kill fully grown caimans.

**Location** South America, Trinidad

**Habitat** 🌿🌱≈🌳

**Diet** Mammals, reptiles

**Status** Least Concern

**Length** 20–33 ft (6–10 m)

Eyes and nostrils are near the top of the head, enabling the snake to see and breathe while its body is under the cover of water.

After a big dinner, an anaconda doesn't need food for months.

The green anaconda's powerful body is strong enough to suffocate animals up to the size of a horse. It often ambushes its victims as they arrive to drink.

# Powerful jaws

What **animal** is this?

What does it **eat**?

How **long** can it grow?

Why was it **endangered**?

How long do its eggs **incubate**?

How does a **baby** inside the egg alert its mother?

**Reptiles**
*Alligator mississippiensis*

# American alligator

Once widely hunted for its skin, the American alligator became seriously endangered in the 1950s, but under legal protection has gained a strong recovery. A powerful reptile, it is black with a broad head, and has a heavily plated back. It also has a large fourth tooth that fits into a socket in the upper jaw.

Location US

Habitat 〰〰

Diet Mammals, fish

Status Least Concern

Length 9¼–16ft (2.8–5m)

An alligator grows replacement teeth for those lost. It can go through 3,000 teeth in its lifetime!

After two months of incubation, warmed by the heat from a nest of decomposing plants, an American alligator is ready to hatch. It yelps while still inside the egg to alert the mother.

The American alligator prefers to float, partially submerged, in lakes, swamps, and marshes. At times, it lies on the shore to bask in the sun.

# Snapping surprise

What **animal** is this?

Where does it **live**?

What is its natural **habitat**?

How does it eat its **prey** when it can't chew?

Is it a **social** creature?

How does it **breathe** when in the water?

**Reptiles**
*Crocodylus niloticus*

# Nile crocodile

The Nile crocodile dwells in large rivers, lakes, and swamps, and is also found in estuaries and river mouths. It feeds on fish, antelope, zebras, and even buffaloes, leaping up to snatch nesting birds or pull drinking animals into the water. Although solitary by nature, several Nile crocodiles gather to catch prey.

**Location** Africa

**Habitat**

**Diet** Mammals, fish, birds

**Status** Least Concern

**Length** 11–20 ft (3.5–6 m)

The Nile crocodile has teeth that are exposed even when its mouth is closed. Like other crocodiles, it can bite but it cannot chew. To solve this problem it drags its prey underwater, and spins around to tear off chunks of flesh.

A Nile crocodile has highly acidic stomach juices that can even digest hooves.

With its eyes and nostrils on the top of its head, the Nile crocodile can see and breathe while partially submerged in water. Its powerful tail and webbed hind feet help it swim.

# Sharp-beaked

What **animal** is this?

What does it **eat**?

Why has it been so widely **hunted**?

What are the **plates** on its back called?

Is this animal **endangered**?

What **distance** can the female travel to lay eggs?

**Reptiles**
*Eretmochelys imbricata*

# Hawksbill turtle

One of the smallest marine turtles, the hawksbill turtle is easily recognized by its carapace (shell). Seen closely, its scutes are beautifully marked—the reason why this species has been so widely hunted. They use their narrow beaks to forage for sponges, mollusks, and other animals on the seabed and among coral reefs.

**Location** Atlantic Ocean, Pacific Ocean

**Habitat** 〰〰

**Diet** Mollusks, sponges

**Status** Critically Endangered

**Length** 23½–32 in (60–80 cm)

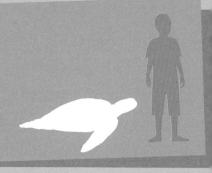

Turtle shells have two parts, the carapace (upper shell) and the plastron (lower shell). Both are constructed of flat, fused bones and covered by wide plates called scutes.

This turtle is named for its sharp, beaklike mouth, which it uses to defend itself.

Only the females ever visit land, crawling up chosen beaches to dig holes and lay their eggs. They may travel thousands of miles to reach these egg-laying grounds.

# Ferocious appearance

What **animal** is this?

Where in the **world** does it live?

What is its natural **habitat**?

How does it **lure** its prey?

How much can it **weigh**?

Is it a **picky** eater?

# Alligator snapping turtle

In folklore, the alligator snapping turtle was thought to be a cross between a common turtle and an alligator. It is ferocious both in appearance and in its habits. When fishing for prey, the animal lies motionless on the river bed, with its mouth wide open. It will eat practically anything it can catch.

**Location** US

**Habitat** 🌿≈ ≈

**Diet** Fish, snails, clams

**Status** Vulnerable

**Length** 16–32 in (40–80 cm)

The alligator snapping turtle is one of the largest freshwater turtles in the world and can weigh up to 200 lb (91 kg).

A single snap of this turtle's beak is strong enough to slice through a broom handle!

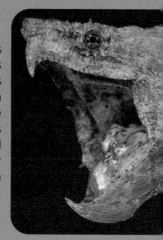

During the day, this turtle lies with its jaws open and lures fish by wriggling a wormlike structure on the floor of its mouth. The hooked upper and lower beaks deliver a powerful bite.

# Gigantic grazer

What **animal** is this?

What is its **diet**?

Is it **endangered**?

What is the name for its **shell**?

Is it a **social** animal?

Where in the **world** does this animal live?

How is it **adapted** to having an unreliable food supply?

**Reptiles**
*Chelonoidis elephantopus*

# Galapagos tortoise

The Galapagos tortoise, the largest living tortoise, has a huge carapace, massive limbs, and a long neck. The overall size and shell shape can vary depending on which of the Galapagos Islands the tortoise originates from. They spend most of their time grazing in small herds and basking in pools.

**Location** Galapagos Islands

**Habitat**

**Diet** Grass, leaves, cacti

**Status** Vulnerable

**Length** Up to 4 ft (1.2 m)

The Galapagos tortoise has strong, toothless jaws well adapted to feeding on any type of vegetation it can find, including tough cacti.

A hatched baby tortoise emerges with the characteristic pattern of scutes on its shell.

The tortoise is adapted to living in an environment with an unreliable food supply—the bigger its body, the more nutrients it can store.

# Poisonous skin

What **animal** is this?

Where does it **live**?

What is its natural **habitat**?

How **long** does this animal grow?

Where in the body does it produce the most **poison**?

Where does it spend the **winter**?

When is it most **active**?

# Fire salamander

The dazzling color scheme of this European fire salamander warns snakes, birds, and other predators that its skin is covered with a poisonous fluid. Most of the poison is produced by glands behind its eyes and on its back. Many other salamanders have similar defenses and are just as colorful.

**Location** Europe

**Habitat** 🌳

**Diet** Worms, slugs, insects

**Status** Least Concern

**Length** 7–11 in (18–28 cm)

The fire salamander is active mainly at night, especially after rain, when it emerges from beneath logs and stones to feed on worms, slugs, insects, and insect larvae.

A fire salamander spends the winter months underground, in a cozy hole.

# Spine-covered skin

What **animal** is this?

What is this animal's natural **habitat**?

What does it **eat**?

Does it always live in **water**?

How does it absorb **oxygen** underwater?

What does it do when it is **threatened**?

When is it most **active**?

**Amphibians**
*Bufo bufo*

# European common toad

The European common toad has a spine-covered skin. Its color ranges from green to brick-red, and females are generally larger than males, particularly in early spring when they are carrying eggs. At this time of year, males and females pair up together in ponds. The female lays eggs around underwater plants.

**Location** Africa, Asia, Europe

**Habitat**

**Diet** Small invertebrates

**Status** Least Concern

**Length** 3¼–8 in (8–20 cm)

The toad spends much of its time away from water, feeding on small animals. It is active at night, hiding by day under logs and in other damp places.

When threatened, the toad stands on tiptoe to make itself look larger.

A toad can absorb oxygen under water through its warty skin.

# Parachuting leaper

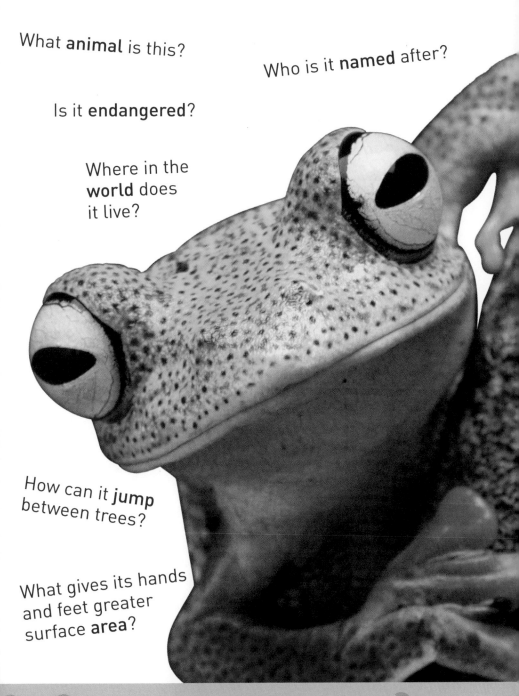

What **animal** is this?

Who is it **named** after?

Is it **endangered**?

Where in the **world** does it live?

How can it **jump** between trees?

What gives its hands and feet greater surface **area**?

**Amphibians**
*Rhacophorus nigropalmatus*

# Wallace's flying frog

Wallace's flying frog is named after its discoverer, Alfred Russel Wallace, the English naturalist who, with Charles Darwin, shares the credit for the theory of evolution by natural selection. This large frog has heavily webbed hands and feet. The limbs have additional narrow ridges that increase their surface area.

**Location** Asia

**Habitat**

**Diet** Small invertebrates

**Status** Least Concern

**Length** 2¾–4in (7–10cm)

A tree frog has sticky pads on each toe which help it cling to glossy leaves.

The large webbed feet of Wallace's flying frog act like parachutes as it leaps from tree to tree. This slows its descent so the frog can travel greater distances.

# Bright eyes

What **animal** is this?

Where does this animal **live**?

What is this animal's natural **habitat**?

What does it **eat**?

How does a male **attract** a female?

How does it **camouflage** itself in the day?

# Red-eyed tree frog

Red-eyed tree frogs are easy to recognize, thanks to their startling coloring. Their bright eyes are thought to surprise predators and discourage them from attacking. However, during the day they often keep their eyes shut, relying on their green skin to camouflage them among forest leaves.

**Location** Central America

**Habitat**

**Diet** Insects

**Status** Least Concern

**Length** 1½–2¾ in (4–7 cm)

In the breeding season, males gather on branches overhanging a pond, and call out to females with a series of clicks.

This frog has a green body, and the insides of its legs are red and yellow. By day, it rests on leaves, with its legs folded to hide all the bright parts of its body.

A second of hesitation from a predator allows the tree frog to leap to safety.

# Forest jouster

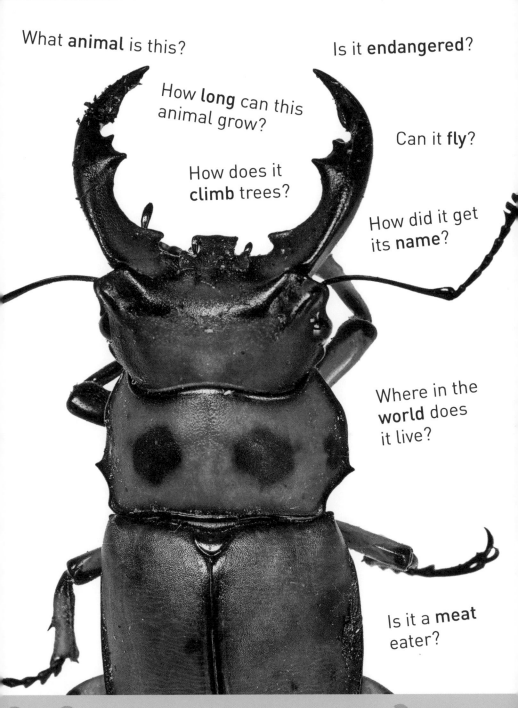

What **animal** is this?

Is it **endangered**?

How **long** can this animal grow?

Can it **fly**?

How does it **climb** trees?

How did it get its **name**?

Where in the **world** does it live?

Is it a **meat** eater?

# Stag beetle

This forest insect is known for the enormous mandibles of the male, which are used in jousting fights. They resemble the antlers of male deer, hence the name stag beetle. Females are smaller than the males, and although their mandibles are more discreet, they can grip more strongly than the males.

**Location** Europe

**Habitat** 🌳🌲

**Diet** Dead wood, sap, fruit juices

**Status** Near Threatened

**Length** ¼–3¼ in (0.6–9 cm)

A stag beetle's legs have hooked claws that help it climb tree bark.

Despite their large size, stag beetles fly frequently. The males fly more often than the females, as they patrol their territories.

Their mandibles have a series of prongs that give a good grip as the fighters try to flip their rival onto its back.

# Powerful limbs

What **animal** is this?

How did it get its **name**?

What is its natural **habitat**?

What does this animal **eat**?

How does it **catch** its prey?

How **long** is this animal?

**Insects**
*Mantis religiosa*

# Common praying mantis

The common praying mantis gets its name from the way it perches on plants with its powerful, spiny front limbs held up as if in prayer. In fact, the mantis uses these to trap its victims and hold them in a deadly grip while it devours them. A hungry praying mantis may even catch and eat other mantises.

**Location** Europe

**Habitat**

**Diet** Moths, crickets, grasshoppers, flies

**Status** Least Concern

**Length** 6 in (15 cm)

A praying mantis bites off the heads of its prey and then eats them.

A praying mantis normally moves very slowly, relying on camouflage to conceal it from prey. It waits for an insect to stray within range, then shoots out its forelimbs to seize it in a spiny trap. The jaws of a mantis are small but very sharp. They can easily chew through an insect's tough exoskeleton.

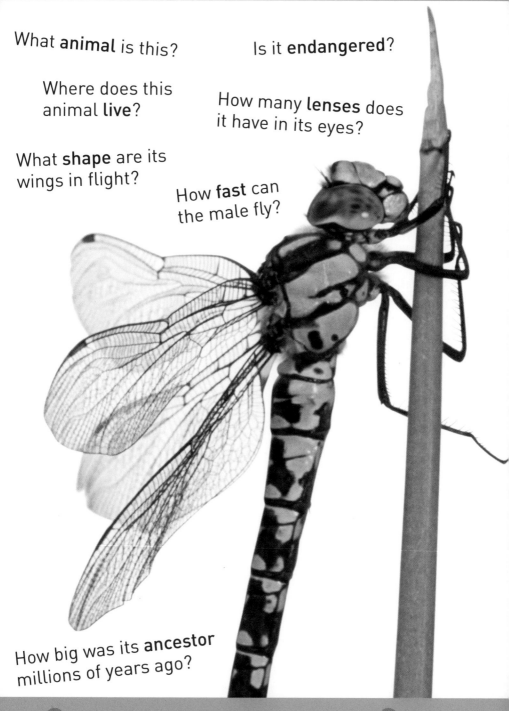

What **animal** is this?

Is it **endangered**?

Where does this animal **live**?

How many **lenses** does it have in its eyes?

What **shape** are its wings in flight?

How **fast** can the male fly?

How big was its **ancestor** millions of years ago?

# Southern hawker dragonfly

Millions of years ago, human-size dragonflies patrolled the skies. Even today's finger-length dragonflies are quite large compared to other insects. The southern hawker dragonfly is a powerful flier. The males fly at speeds of up to 19 mph (30 kph) when competing with other males over their breeding territories.

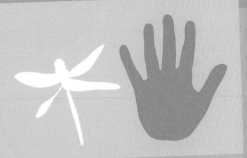

**Location** Europe

**Habitat** 🌾≈≈≈

**Diet** Tadpoles, young fish

**Status** Least Concern

**Length** 2½–3½ in (6.5–9 cm)

A dragonfly's spiny legs are so specialized for seizing prey that it cannot walk.

Dragonflies have excellent eyesight. They have two huge compound eyes, each with up to 30,000 lenses.

Dragonflies have strong muscles which control the base of the wings. In flight, the wings look like a rapidly changing X shape.

# Record breaker

What **animal** is this?

What does it **eat**?

What is its natural **habitat**?

What is its **wingspan**?

Is it a **social** creature?

How **far** can it fly?

Where does it **migrate** to in winter?

# Monarch butterfly

Some butterflies are capable of amazingly long flights—the monarch holds the distance record. Each fall they fly south from North America in search of food and warmth. They reproduce and eventually die, with later generations making the journey home. The monarch may fly 3,000 miles (4,800 km).

**Location** The Americas, Oceania

**Habitat**

**Diet** Nectar, milkweed foliage

**Status** Not Evaluated

**Length** Wingspan up to 4¼ in (11 cm)

In winter vast numbers of monarch butterflies gather in the warm woodlands of California and Mexico. They stay for more than four months, sleeping in clusters on favored trees, before heading north again to breed.

Bright orange-colored wings warn birds that the butterflies are toxic.

# Deadly fly

What **animal** is this?

How does the female **find** its prey?

How is it **dangerous** to humans?

What is its **diet**?

Where does the female lay **eggs**?

How **long** is this animal?

Where does this animal **live**?

When is it most **active**?

# Malaria mosquito

The most deadly animal on Earth is not a killer shark or a venomous snake, but a small fly with a harmful bite—the malaria mosquito. The parasites that it carries in its body can infect a victim's red blood cells, causing a fatal fever. The malaria mosquito is responsible for at least a million human deaths every year.

**Location** Africa

**Habitat**

**Diet** Nectar, blood

**Status** Not Evaluated

**Length** Up to ¼ in (8mm)

A mosquito's mouthparts can detect a vein beneath the skin.

The female flies mainly by night, and finds her victims by detecting their breath and body heat. She can often bite without being detected, allowing her to drink her fill of a victim's blood. After a meal, the abdomen fills with eggs over two to three days. The eggs are then laid in water.

# Busy buzzer

What **animal** is this?

Is it a **social** creature?

What is its **nest** made from?

What is its natural **habitat**?

Is it **hairy**?

How does it make a **noise**?

Is this animal **endangered**?

# Buff-tailed bumblebee

Bumblebees are incredibly active insects and can visit several thousand flowers a day. As they weave their way between blooms, their rapidly beating wings make a buzzing sound. Bumblebees have spread around the world. They have adapted to a huge range of habitats and become spectacularly diverse.

**Location** Africa, Asia, Europe

**Habitat**

**Diet** Nectar

**Status** Least Concern

**Length** ⅛–1 in (0.3–2.7 cm)

A buff-tailed bumblebee usually nests in the ground.

Like all its relatives, the buff-tailed bumblebee has a body covered by "fur," enabling it to fly in the cool conditions of early spring.

Bees are social insects, living in complex colonies consisting of a queen, males, and sterile female workers. Their nests are made of grass with wax cells.

# Farmer's friend

What **animal** is this?

Where does this animal **live**?

What is its **nest** made from?

What does it **eat**?

How is it **helpful** to farmers?

How **long** is this animal?

What does it feed its **larvae**?

# Common wasp

Many species of wasps are useful to farmers because they kill the grubs and caterpillars that destroy crops. The common wasp is a helpful garden species because it removes caterpillars and other pests. It has bright yellow and black markings to warn other insects that it has a painful sting. Its stinger can be used repeatedly.

**Location** Worldwide (except Antarctica)

**Habitat** 🌳 🌲 🌴 🌿 🏡

**Diet** Nectar, honeydew

**Status** Not Evaluated

**Length** $^{5}/_{32}$–1½ in (0.4–3.6 cm)

A wasp has some hair, but is much smoother than a bee.

Common wasps scrape wood fibers from trees to make paper for their nests. They live in colonies inside their rounded paper nests and catch insects, often caterpillars, to feed to their larvae.

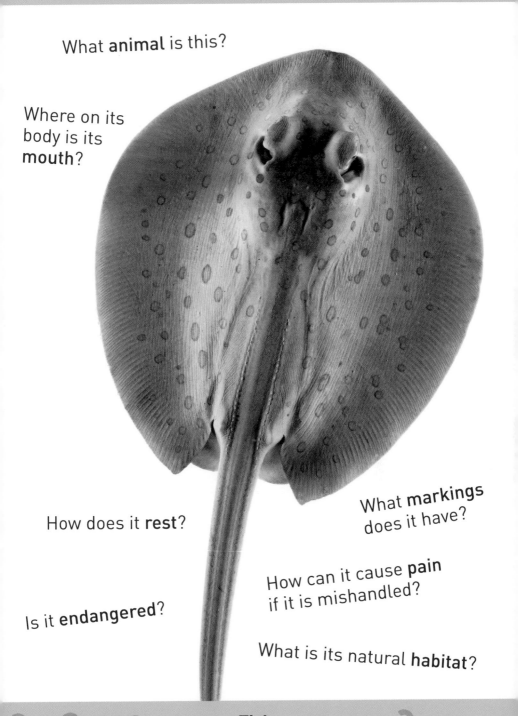

What **animal** is this?

Where on its body is its **mouth**?

How does it **rest**?

What **markings** does it have?

How can it cause **pain** if it is mishandled?

Is it **endangered**?

What is its natural **habitat**?

**Fish**
*Taeniura lymma*

# Blue-spotted stingray

One of the handsomest members of the stingray family, this species has blue spots scattered over its body. In addition, it has blue stripes along the side of its tail and a lighter underside. Like all stingrays, this fish has a toxic spine at the base of its tail and can inflict a nasty sting if stepped on or mishandled.

**Location** Indian Ocean, Pacific Ocean

**Habitat**

**Diet** Small fish, invertebrates

**Status** Near Threatened

**Length** Up to 6½ft (2m)

Blue-spotted stingrays rest with their bodies largely hidden by mud or sand, with just their eyes projecting above the surface. In shallow water, hidden rays are easily stepped on.

A stingray's teeth are constantly replaced before they are worn out.

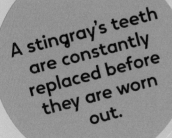

The mouth, nostrils, and gill slits are all on the underside. The skin is plain white.

# Terror of the sea

What **animal** is this?

Is it **endangered**?

How **long** is this animal?

What does it **eat**?

Can it **jump** out of the water?

Why does it sometimes swim with its **teeth** bared?

**Fish**
*Carcharodon carcharias*

# White shark

Also known as the great white shark, this powerful swimmer cruises through the water, either at the surface or just off the bottom, covering long distances quickly. It also excels at short, fast chases, and leaps spectacularly out of the water. Although usually solitary, it may be seen in pairs or small groups.

**Location** Warm oceans

**Habitat** 

**Diet** Fish, seals, cetaceans

**Status** Vulnerable

**Length** 20–26ft (6–8m)

A shark's nose can detect electrical signals generated by animals' muscles.

Armed with its large, coarsely serrated teeth, the white shark is superbly equipped to rip into the flesh of its unfortunate prey. This shark has been known to swim along with its teeth bared, which may warn off competitors for food, or intruding rival sharks.

# Striped danger

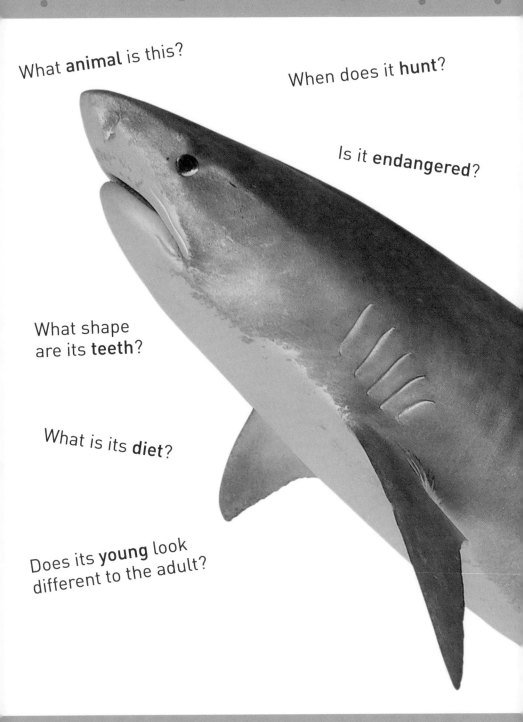

What **animal** is this?

When does it **hunt**?

Is it **endangered**?

What shape
are its **teeth**?

What is its **diet**?

Does its **young** look
different to the adult?

**Fish**
*Galeocerdo cuvier*

# Tiger shark

The tiger shark is one of the world's most dangerous sharks. It has distinctive teeth shaped like a cockerel's comb, and a head that is disproportionately large for its slender, streamlined body. This shark generally prefers coastal waters, often moving inshore to feed at night.

**Location** Warm oceans

**Habitat**

**Diet** Almost anything

**Status** Near Threatened

**Length** 18–25ft (5.5–7.5m)

A primarily nocturnal hunter, the tiger shark has the most indiscriminate diet among sharks. It employs quick bursts of speed to catch live prey, such as fish and reptiles, invertebrates, and mammals. It also scavenges on carrion, and may even feed on trash.

A tiger shark can grab a seabird from the surface of the sea.

Young sharks of this species are marked with vertical, tigerlike stripes. These may fade or be absent in adults.

# Unusual fish

What **animal** is this?

How **long** can it be?

How can this animal be **recognized** easily?

What helps it **camouflage** itself?

Where in the water does it **live**?

The **female** carries her eggs. True or false?

**Fish**
*Phyllopteryx taeniolatus*

# Weedy sea dragon

The weedy or common sea dragon is one of the largest seahorses, and one of the most bizarrely shaped. Its body is covered with toughened plates, and leaflike flaps help provide camouflage. Usually found just above the seabed, the weedy sea dragon hides among seaweed and plants growing on rocky reefs.

**Location** Australia

**Habitat** 〰〰

**Diet** Small invertebrates

**Status** Least Concern

**Length** Up to 18in (46cm)

After mating takes place, the fertilized eggs are attached to the male's tail and carried around by him. As the eggs hatch, the baby sea dragons swim away.

A weedy sea dragon cannot coil its tail around objects, unlike other seahorses.

The sea dragon searches for small invertebrates, including shrimp, among weeds and sponges near the ocean floor.

# Spiny ball

What **animal** is this?

How does it **protect** itself when it is threatened?

Why doesn't it have **spines** that stand on end all the time?

What is this animal's natural **habitat**?

How do its **babies** avoid predators?

What does it **eat**?

What **color** is it?

**Fish**
*Diodon holocanthus*

# Long-spine porcupine fish

When the long-spine porcupine fish is threatened, it swallows large amounts of water, inflating itself until it becomes almost spherical. Its spines stand on end to protect it, but the spiny armor may restrict its ability to swim. Long-spine porcupine fish are brown above and yellow below.

**Location** Warm oceans

**Habitat** 〰️ 🪸

**Diet** Snails, sea urchins, crabs

**Status** Least Concern

**Length** Up to 20 in (50 cm)

Baby porcupine fish hide from big predators by using their dark patches to disguise them among fronds of seaweed.

A porcupine fish can swallow water to expand to 3–4 times its normal size.

Its spines lie flat when the fish is swimming normally, but stick out when it puffs up.

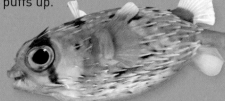

What **animal** is this?

How **long** is it?

Is it **endangered**?

Where in the **world** does this animal live?

What can it **eat** that many other fish can't?

What **markings** does it have as an adult?

Where does it usually **live**?

**Fish**
*Pomacanthus imperator*

# Emperor angelfish

The angelfish is among the most flamboyant inhabitants of coral reefs, with intense colors and bold patterns on its body. The emperor angelfish has a small mouth with comblike teeth. Rare among fish, it has the ability to digest the tough flesh of sponges, which are abundant on coral reefs.

**Location** Indian Ocean, Pacific Ocean

**Habitat** 〜〜 🪸

**Diet** Sponges, sea squirts

**Status** Least Concern

**Length** Up to 16 in (40 cm)

Angelfish are dependent on the shelter of boulders, caves, and coral crevices. They normally inhabit areas with heavy coral growth or substantial rock formations.

Young angelfish have a completely different pattern than the adults.

Adults have yellow and purple stripes on the body. On the head and around the pectoral fin are light blue, dark blue, and black markings.

What **animal** is this?

In what ocean does it **live**?

How can this animal **climb**?

How does it **breathe** out of water?

Does it **move** faster in or out of the water?

What does it do if it gets too **dry**?

What is this animal's natural **habitat**?

**Fish**
*Periophthalmus barbarus*

# Atlantic mudskipper

Special fins allow the Atlantic mudskipper to walk, jump, and climb as well as swim. In fact, the mudskipper moves faster on land—where it hunts for insects to eat—than in water. Most of its time is spent out of water, so it needs to keep its skin moist. When it gets too dry, it rolls in puddles, and wipes its face with a wet fin.

**Location** Atlantic Ocean

**Habitat**

**Diet** Small animals

**Status** Least Concern

**Length** Up to 10 in (25 cm)

A mudskipper can roll its eyes back into its sockets to keep them moist.

To breathe on land, the Atlantic mudskipper fills the spaces around its gills with water. These spaces keep the fish supplied with oxygen while it is on dry land.

# Fearsome teeth

What **animal** is this?

How **long** can it grow?

How does it **detect** prey?

When does it **feed**?

Is this a **solitary** creature?

Where in the **world** does this animal live?

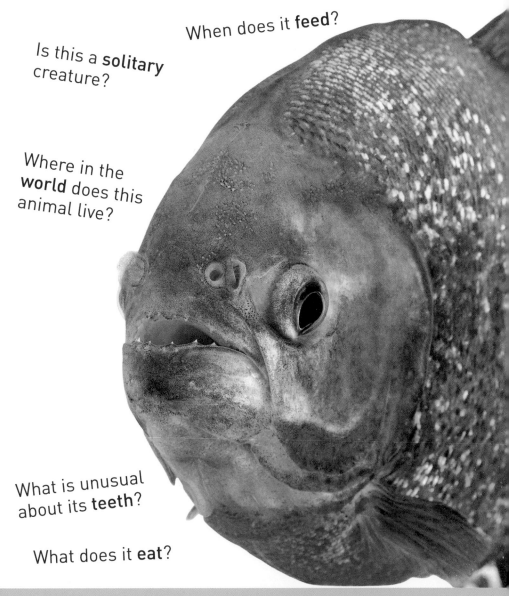

What is unusual about its **teeth**?

What does it **eat**?

**Fish**
*Pygocentrus nattereri*

# Red piranha

Notorious for their predatory, pack-feeding behavior, red piranhas typically feed at dawn and dusk, lurking and then dashing at their prey. They generally eat animals smaller than themselves. However, given an opportunity, these extremely aggressive predators can kill much larger prey by hunting as a group.

**Location** South America

**Habitat** 〰

**Diet** Insects, fish, mammals

**Status** Not Evaluated

**Length** Up to 20 in (50 cm)

The red piranha has sharp teeth set in powerful jaws. The teeth interlock when the mouth shuts, allowing it to rip off chunks of flesh. The hanging lower jaw also helps it bite with unusual force.

Mass red piranha attacks can kill animals as large as capybaras and horses.

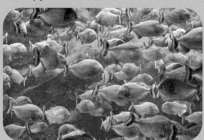

A piranha can sense its prey with pressure detectors on its flanks.

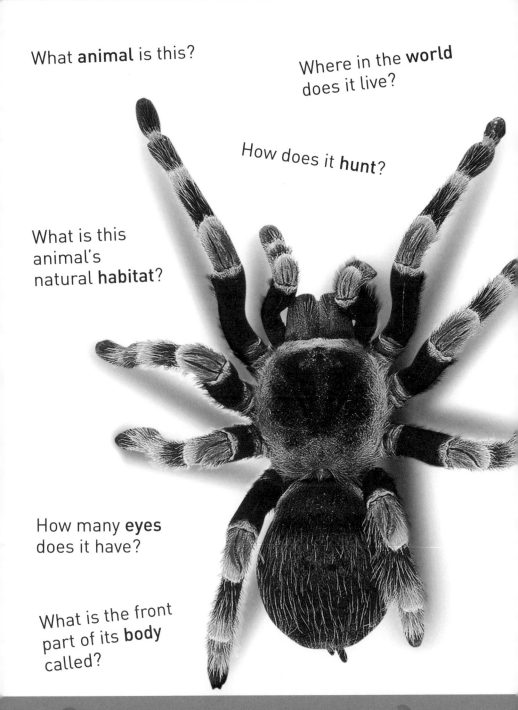

What **animal** is this?

Where in the **world** does it live?

How does it **hunt**?

What is this animal's natural **habitat**?

How many **eyes** does it have?

What is the front part of its **body** called?

# Mexican red-knee tarantula

Tarantulas are spiders with big, hairy bodies, which typically prey on large insects. One of the biggest spiders, the Mexican red-knee tarantula is an ambush hunter that pounces on small animals wandering near its burrow at night. Darting out, the spider seizes its victim and injects a paralyzing venom with its fangs.

**Location** Mexico

**Habitat**

**Diet** Small animals, large insects

**Status** Near Threatened

**Length** Up to 4in (10cm)

A tarantula's hinged, jawlike structures mash prey to a pulp.

The Mexican red-knee tarantula has eight small eyes on top of its body, but cannot see in detail and relies on its other senses to detect prey.

The body has two main sections, joined by a narrow waist. The bulbous rear part is called the abdomen. The front part (prosoma) combines the head and thorax.

# Sting in the tail

What **animal** is this?

How **long** is this animal?

What does it **eat**?

Where does it **live**?

How does it appear under **UV** light?

What do its **young** look like?

When does it **hunt**?

# Emperor scorpion

Armed with an enormous pair of pincers and a sting in its tail, the emperor scorpion prowls the forest floor at night in search of prey. One of the biggest scorpions, it hunts almost entirely by touch, sensing the movement of prey by detecting vibrations in the ground. Scorpions are arachnids—relatives of spiders.

**Location** Africa

**Habitat**

**Diet** Small animals

**Status** Not Evaluated

**Length** Up to 8 in (20 cm)

A scorpion sheds its tough exoskeleton several times as it grows.

Scorpions give birth to tiny, pale-skinned replicas of their parents, complete with stings. When the young are born, the mother carries them around on her back until they can fend for themselves.

The exoskeleton contains chemicals that make it glow a bright green-blue under ultraviolet light.

# Quick-witted hunter

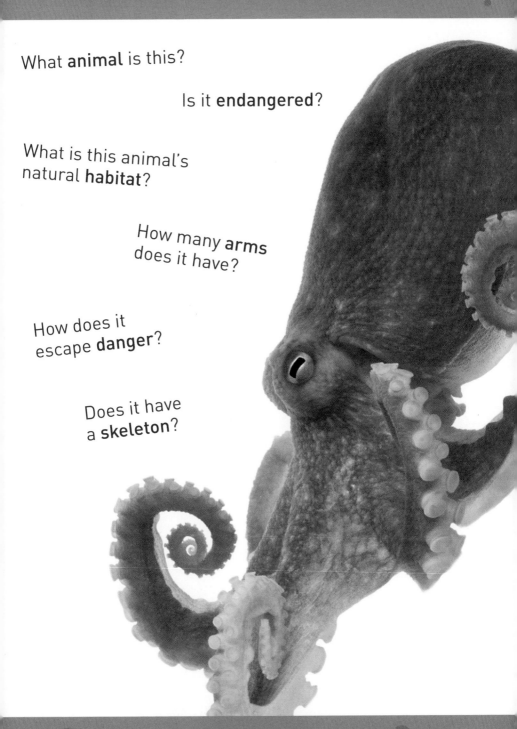

What **animal** is this?

Is it **endangered**?

What is this animal's natural **habitat**?

How many **arms** does it have?

How does it escape **danger**?

Does it have a **skeleton**?

**Invertebrates**
*Octopus vulgaris*

# Common octopus

The common octopus is a quick-witted hunter and one of the most intelligent of all invertebrates. Its eight arms are used for crawling and hunting, while its powerful beak can crack through tough shells. With no internal skeleton or outer shell, an octopus is able to squeeze its entire body through narrow openings.

**Location** Worldwide

**Habitat**

**Diet** Clams, shrimp, lobsters, fish, sharks

**Status** Least Concern

**Length** 3¼ft (1 m)

An octopus has blue blood and three hearts!

An octopus can use water-jet propulsion to escape danger. It fills the mantle with water and then squeezes it back out, pushing itself forward. For extra protection, it releases a jet of dark ink that hides the octopus as it shoots away.

# Home swapper

What **animal** is this?

What is its natural **habitat**?

Where in the **world** does it live?

What is its **diet**?

How does it **protect** itself?

How does it **move** along?

**Invertebrates**
*Dardanus megistos*

# White-spotted hermit crab

Unlike most crabs, the white-spotted hermit crab has a long, soft body. It must protect it by living in the empty shell of a sea snail, where it can tuck its body away. The crab can stretch its legs out of the shell to pull itself along. Hermit crabs carry the shells around as homes, swapping for a bigger one as they grow.

**Location** Atlantic, Indian, Pacific oceans

**Habitat**

**Diet** Algae, tube worms, fish

**Status** Not Evaluated

**Length** 5–8in (13–20cm)

A female crab lays millions of eggs, but only a handful survive.

When the crab grows too big for one shell, it must move out to find a larger one (shown here). It pokes its claws into empty shells to see if they are large enough.

# Bristly tentacles

What **animal** is this?

Is it **poisonous**?

Where does this animal **live**?

Is this animal **endangered**?

How **long** can it grow?

What can it do if **attacked**?

How does it use its **tentacles**?

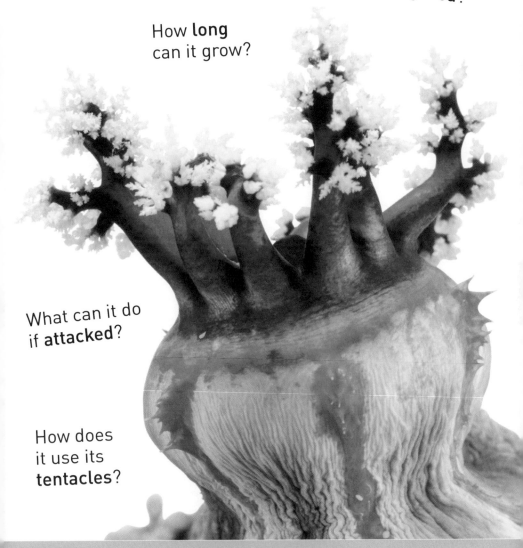

# Sea apple cucumber

The slow-moving sea apple cucumber lives on the seafloor. Its bright colors are a warning that it contains poison in its flesh. If that doesn't work, sea apple cucumbers resort to drastic measures. They squirt out their innards in a sticky mess—usually enough to send the hungriest prowler away.

**Location** Worldwide

**Habitat**

**Diet** Plankton, decaying material

**Status** Not Evaluated

**Length** Up to 11 ft (3.3 m)

These sea creatures can regrow their body organs within two weeks.

The bristly tentacles around the mouth of a sea cucumber are extra-long tube feet. They are used like sticky fingers to trap food particles floating by and feed them into the body.

# Slow glider

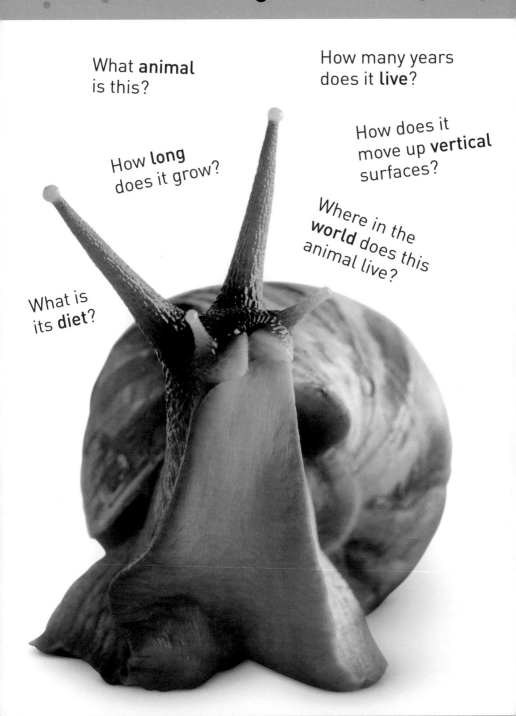

What **animal** is this?

How many years does it **live**?

How **long** does it grow?

How does it move up **vertical** surfaces?

Where in the **world** does this animal live?

What is its **diet**?

# Giant African snail

The giant African snail is the world's biggest land-dwelling snail. Unlike sea snails, land-dwelling snails have thin, relatively light shells. This snail can cause serious damage to agriculture in the areas where it thrives. It's a hardy species that can survive cold or even snowy conditions by hibernating inside its shell.

**Location** Africa, Asia

**Habitat**

**Diet** Leaves

**Status** Not Evaluated

**Length** 1 ft (30 cm)

An African snail's shell provides camouflage by blending into its habitat.

The giant African snail grows to a length of 1 ft (30 cm)—as long as a rabbit. Typically, adults live for five to six years.

The snail contracts its foot muscle in waves, making it creep forward. Glands in the foot release a thick liquid that helps it glide on the ground or stick to vertical surfaces.

# Ancient relic

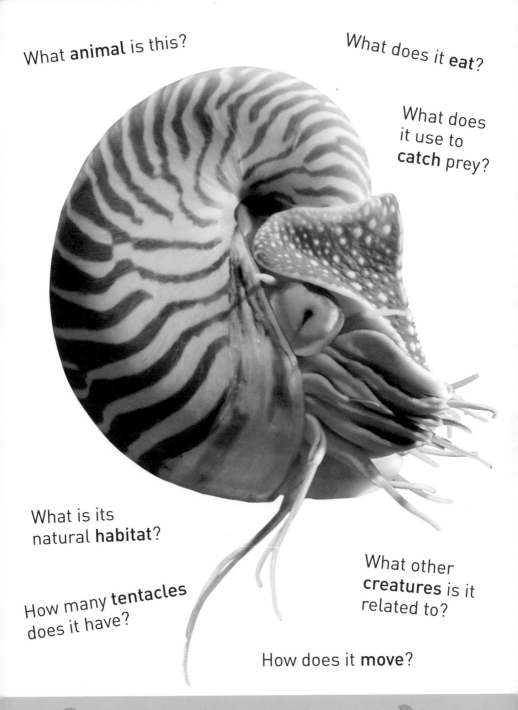

What **animal** is this?

What does it **eat**?

What does it use to **catch** prey?

What is its natural **habitat**?

How many **tentacles** does it have?

What other **creatures** is it related to?

How does it **move**?

# Chambered nautilus

The chambered nautilus shows striking similarities to fossil finds from 400 million years ago—long before the dinosaurs and when almost all complex animal life lived in the oceans. It is a relative of squids and octopuses. The nautilus's shell has gas-filled chambers that help the animal float at the right depth.

**Location** Indian Ocean, Pacific Ocean

**Habitat**

**Diet** Crustaceans, small fish

**Status** Not Evaluated

**Length** 6–9½ in (15–24 cm)

Thin tentacles are attached to the long body of the nautilus. The tentacles grab prey, such as crabs, while the horny beak bites through shells.

A nautilus has 90 small tentacles and pinhole eyes with no lenses.

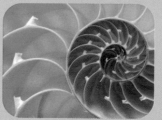

The nautilus lives inside a shell. It uses the air chambers inside it to stay afloat and jet propulsion to move through the ocean.

# Huge claw

What **animal** is this?

Where does it **live**?

What is its **claw** used for?

When is it mostly **active**?

What is this animal's natural **habitat**?

How does it avoid **danger**?

How does it **fight** a rival male?

# Orange fiddler crab

A male orange fiddler crab is easily recognized because one claw is greatly enlarged. This claw makes up more than half the crab's body weight and is used both to attract potential mates and to ward off rival males. If disputes arise, the weaker individual usually retreats before any serious damage is done.

**Location** Indian Ocean, Pacific Ocean

**Habitat** 〰️🌿〰️

**Diet** Sediments

**Status** Not Evaluated

**Length** 1 in (2.5 cm)

Orange fiddler crabs are active during the day. As well as digging a deep main burrow, they create a number of boltholes they can retreat into if danger threatens.

If waving their claws does not scare off a rival male, then two crabs may "arm-wrestle" each other to resolve their dispute.

Fiddler crabs have gills but they obtain oxygen from air not water.

What **animal** is this?

What does it **eat**?

Where does it **live**?

How **long** does
this animal grow?

How does it **see**?

Can it **swim**?

# Blue starfish

Starfish are star-shaped, but they are not fish—they are echinoderms. This means that they have spiny skin. They cannot swim, but they are very good at crawling. They can walk up strands of seaweed and climb down the sides of rocks. Even in the deepest, darkest parts of the sea, there are starfish creeping around.

**Location** Pacific Ocean, Indian Ocean

**Habitat**

**Diet** Small organisms and particles

**Status** Not Evaluated

**Length** Up to 3¼ ft (1 m)

Starfish don't have eyes. Instead, they have eye spots on the tips of their bendy arms. These special cells cannot see shapes, but they can tell whether it is light or dark.

If a starfish arm is torn off, it grows into a new starfish.

The blue starfish belongs to a group of starfish with elongated, snakelike arms. Not all species are blue in color—a minority of individuals are purple or orange.

# Crawling critter

Where in the **world** does this animal live?

What **animal** is this?

What is this animal's natural **habitat**?

What does it do if **threatened**?

How many pairs of **legs** does it have?

Where does it lay its **eggs**?

# White-rimmed pill millipede

Millipedes have between 36 and 450 legs, two pairs growing from each body segment. White-rimmed pill millipedes are a short, squat species, with only 11 to 13 body segments. Adults have 15 pairs of legs. They lay their eggs in soil, and when the young hatch, they initially have only three pairs of legs.

**Location** Africa, Asia, Europe

**Habitat**

**Diet** Dead organic matter

**Status** Not Evaluated

**Length** ¹⁄₁₆–³⁄₄ in (0.2–2 cm)

The shape of the back plates allows the white-rimmed pill millipede to roll into a tight ball if threatened.

White-rimmed pill millipedes have much shorter bodies than other millipedes.

When a millipede walks, a wave of movement ripples down its body.

# Index

# Acknowledgments

For Smithsonian Enterprises
Avery Naughton, Licensing Coordinator; Paige Towler, Editorial Lead; Jill Corcoran, Senior Director, Licensed Publishing; Brigid Ferraro, Vice President of New Business and Licensing; Carol LeBlanc, President

The publisher would like to thank the following for their kind permission to reproduce their photographs:
(Key: a-above; b-below/bottom; c-center; l-left; r-right; Alamy Stock Photo: ASP; DK: Dorling Kindersley; Dreamstime.com: DT; Getty Images: GI; Nature Picture Library, and naturepl.com: NPL; Shutterstock.com: SS)

Tiger: 123RF.com: Daniel Lamborn (l). DT: Eric Isselee (r). DK: Jerry Young. Lion: DT: Ecophoto (cl). Snow leopard: DT: Abeselom Zerit. DK: Wildlife Heritage Foundation, Kent, UK (b). DT: Glenn Nagel (cr). Flying Cordulegaster: DT: Isselee (tr). Jaguar: 123RF. com: Ana Vasileva/ABV. 123RF.com: Johnny Lye (l). Cheetah: iStock: GlobalP. DT: Dennis Donohue/Silksatsunrise (b); Lucasdm (cr). Leopard: DT: Volodymyrkrasyuk (b). Killer whale: 123RF.com: Simone Gatterwe. GI: Michael Weberberger (cl); by wildestanimal (b). Bottlenose dolphin: DT: Neirfy (r). African elephant: 123RF. com: Donovan van Staden. Honey badger: ASP: dpa picture alliance. Black-tailed jackrabbit: ASP: Evelyn Harrison. DT: Derrick Neill. Arctic hare: SS: Edwin Godinho. ASP: NPL (r); Our Wild Life Photography (l). Moose: SS: Gallinago_media. iStock: Freder (r). Reindeer: DT: Simone Winkler/Eyecatchlight; Iakov Filimonov (l). Fotolia: Nadezhda Bolotina (r). Guanaco: DT: Iakov Filimonov. Dromedary: DK: Jerry Young. DT: Valentin Armianu/Asterixvs (r); Bennymarty (l). Sable antelope: ASP: Martin Harvey; Imagebroker (l). DT: Photogallet (r). Northern giraffe: DT: Alejandro Duran. SS: Cathy Withers-Clarke (l). Mountain goat: DT: Iakov Filimonov. GI: Mike Berenson/Colorado Captures. Common Seal: 123RF.com: Eric Isselee. ASP: Life on white (r); David Osborn (l). Walrus: DT: Vladimir Melnik/Zanskar. GI: Paul Souders. Capybara: DK: Gary Ombler/Cotswold Wildlife Park. DT: Amaiquez (r). California sea lion: ASP: Laura Romin & Larry Dalton; Oliver Smart (cb). Bornean orangutan: DT: Neurobite; Dejan Stojaković (l); Sergey Uryadnikov (r) Common chimpanzee: 123RF.com: Eric Isselee. SS: Sergey Uryadnikov (r). Ring-tailed lemur: Fotolia: Eric Isselee. ASP: macana (l). SS: Wang LiQiang (r). American bison: iStock: VladGans. DT: Chase Dekker (cb). iStock: gkuchera (b). Blue wildebeest: 123RF.com: mhgallery. ASP: Martin Harvey. Cape springbok: 123RF.com: bennymarty. ASP: Imagebroker (r). DT: Johannes Gerhardus Swanepoel/Johan63 (l). Meerkat: GI: Martin Harvey (cl). SS: anetapics (b). African wild dog: SS: GoodFocused. ASP: Cindy Hopkins (r). DK: Jerry Young (l). Grey wolf: ASP: Jim Cumming. DT: Maria Itina (r). iStock: alexandrumagurean (l). Arctic fox: ASP: Life on white. DK: Jerry Young (r). GI: Natphotos (l). Northern raccoon: ASP: Imagebroker (r). Virginia opossum: 123RF.com: Marion Wear/mawear. SS: Sari ONeal. Tasmanian devil: ASP: Imagebroker; Ian Watt. Koala: DT: Isselee. 123RF.com: Eric Isselee (l). DT: Ongchangwei (r). Red kangaroo: ASP: Bradley Blackburn. 123RF.com: smileus (r). GI: Marianne Purdie (l). Eurasian red squirrel: DT: Isselee. 123RF.com: Eric Isselee (r); Anatolii Tsekhmister (l). American beaver: DT: Musat Christian, SS: Chase Dekker. Chilean chinchilla: SS: Seregraff (r). Narwhal: iStock: Vac1 (b). ASP: All Canada Photos (a). Humpback whale: SS: Yann hubert. SS: Gudkov Andrey (l); Jay Ondreicka (r). Beluga: SS: svrid79. DT: Wei Chuan Liu (cb). SS: Miles Away Photography (b). Vampire bat: ASP: NPL. DK: Jerry Young (b). Polar bear: 123RF.com: Eric Isselee. DT: Sergey Uryadnikov (r). GI: sergei gladyshev (l). Giant panda: 123RF.com: Eric Isselee. Fotolia: Eric Isselee (b). SS: Bryan Faust (cb). Brown bear: SS: Chase Dekker; Alexey Suloev (r). Plains zebra: SS: olga_gl (r). Przewalski's horse: iStock: vapno. SS: Shyrochenko Aleksandr. Black rhino: SS: gualtiero boffi, Rob Francis (cb); TashaBubo (b). Ground pangolin: SS: dwi putra stock. ASP: Natural History Media (b). SS: dwi putra stock (cb). Giant anteater: ASP: Life on white, Life on white (l). SS: GR92100 (r). Southern two-toed sloth: SS: Eric Isselee; Petr Simon. Nine banded armadillo: ASP: Minden Pictures;

Imagebroker (r, l). Moholi bush baby: SS: EcoPrint (l). ASP: NPL (r). Common Hippopotamus: SS: Eric Isselee; Henk Bogaard (cb); jesterpop (b). Toco toucan: SS: asharkyu. DT: John Caezar Panelo/ Jcpsad (r). SS: Humberto Mancuso (l). Great spotted woodpecker: SS: John Navajo. SS: Kristyna Henkeova (r); Tobyphotos (l). Indian peacock: SS: Guan jiangchi. DT: Shawn Hempel (cb). White-Backed vulture: SS: Henner Damke (l); Dmussman (r). Scarlet ibis: SS: Alfredo Maiquez; Anton Harder (l); YuriFineart (r). Common kingfisher: SS: Butterfly Hunter. DT: Rudmer Zwerver. Mute swan: 123RF.com: NewAge. 190 SS: Nabichi (cb); Jonas Vegele (b). Laughing kookaburra: SS: Ken Griffiths (r). DT: Steve Byland (l). Ruby-throated hummingbird: SS: Agnieszka Bacal. Common ostrich: SS: Eric Isselee. ASP: Ariadne Van Zandbergen (r). SS: Krakenimages.com (l). North Island brown kiwi: DT: Eric Isselee. ASP: Minden Pictures (l). SS: Eric Isselee (r). Snowy owl: SS: Jim Cumming. NPL: Markus Varesvuo (l). SS: Jim Cumming (r). Bald eagle: iStock: igorkov. DT: Lawrence Weslowski Jr (l). SS: IDTPhoto (r). Red-fan parrot: SS: Eric Isselee. Sulfur-crested cockatoo: iStock: GlobalP. SS: KarenHBlack (r); Gayamal Rathnavibushana (l). Atlantic puffin: DT: Isselee. ASP: blickwinkel (l). iStock: Henk Bogaard (r). Common cuckoo: SS: Simon C Stobart; Daniel Prudek. Greater flamingo: SS: Amani A (l); Ondrej Prosicky (r). Peregrine falcon: DK: Frank Greenaway/ National Birds of Prey Centre, Gloucestershire. ASP: Nathan Guttridge (r). DT: Ken Griffiths (l). Great egret: DT: Byvalet. DT: Martha Marks (r); Howard Nevitt, Jr.m (l). Barn swallow: 123RF. com: Eric Isselee. DT: Mikelane45 (r); Oleksandr Panchenko (l). Emperor penguin: DT: Kotomiti_okuma. NPL: Stefan Christmann. Marine iguana: DT: Donyanedomam. SS: Uwe Bergwitz (r); sunsinger (l). Frilled lizard: SS: PetlinDmitry. Komodo dragon: SS: Anna Kucherova, Sergey Uryadnikov. Green iguana: SS: chrisbrignell; Avroracoon (cb). Gila monster: SS: fivespots; Eric Isselee (cb); reptiles4all (b). Jackson's chameleon: SS: Eric Isselee. DT: Kcmatt. King cobra: NPL: Daniel Heuclin (cb). SS: reptiles4all (b). Green anaconda: SS: Vladimir Wrangel (r). American alligator: SS: Eric Isselee; Heiko Kiera (cb); Ondrej Prosicky (b). Nile crocodile: DK: Jerry Young (b). SS: Enrique Ramos (cb). Hawksbill turtle: SS: Rich Carey. iStock: RainervonBrandis (b). SS: blue-sea.cz (cb). Alligator snapping turtle: SS: Faiz Zaki. DT: Faiz Zaki (l); Matthijs Kuijpers (r). Galapagos tortoise: SS: Smileus. DT: Kim Deadman (cb). Fire salamander: SS: Wirestock Creators. European common toad: DT: Isselee. NPL: Jane Burton (b). SS: Marek Mierzejewski (cb). Wallace's flying frog: GI: irawansubingarphotography. ASP: Minden Pictures. Red-eyed tree frog: SS: Dirk Ercken (tc). SS: Dave Denby Photography (b); Peterr R (cb). Stag beetle: SS: Nobra (cb). Common praying mantis: SS: Kaisarmuda. Southern hawker dragonfly: SS: Karolsejnova (l). Monarch butterfly: 123RF. com: Thawat Tanhai. SS: Isabelle OHara. Malaria mosquito: SS: nechaevkon. Common wasp: iStock: imv. Blue-spotted stingray: iStock: Placebo365 (cb). White shark: DT: Nerthuz. Tiger shark: DK: Terry Goss. DT: Naluphoto (cb). SS: Matt9122 (b). Weedy sea dragon: DK: Frank Greenaway/Weymouth Sea Life Centre. iStock: Katherine OBrien (cb). SS: katherineobrien (b). Long-spine porcupine fish: DT: Isselee. DT: Isselee (b). iStock: AndamanSE (cb). Emperor angelfish: iStock: richcarey (r). Atlantic mudskipper: SS: aRTI01 (l). Red piranha: DT: Dennis Jacobsen (l). SS: Mark Green (r). Emperor scorpion: DK: Jerry Young. SS: Dan Olsen (b); tskstock (cb). Common octopus: ASP: Imagebroker. White-spotted hermit crab: SS: speedshutter Photography. Sea apple cucumber: SS: Lindsey Lu. Giant African snail: SS: Oleg Shvydiuk (l). DK: Frank Greenaway/University Marine Biological Station, Millport, Scotland (r). Chambered nautilus: iStock: peilien. ASP: WaterFrame (r). SS: aaltair (l). Orange fiddler crab: NPL: Jane Burton (r). SS: Marut Sayannikroth (r). Blue starfish: SS: Dmitry Rukhlenko (l). White-rimmed pill millipede: SS: Eric Isselee (clb).

All other images © Dorling Kindersley